Dancing on the Graves of Your Past

Yvonne Martinez

DANCING ON THE GRAVES OF YOUR PAST

ISBN 1448626722
EAN-13   9781448626724
Printed in the United States of America

Published and distributed by: Stillwater Lavender
www.StillwaterLavender.com

$\mathcal{D}$EDICATION

Dedicated to my husband and best friend, Tony ~

Your evangelistic heart saw my desperate need for a Savior and you invited me into relationship with the One who would heal all my brokenness.

You remain my rescuer, my hero, my anchor, my lover and friend.

You are the reason I learned to dance on the graves of my past.

It is all your fault!

Thank You

I want to thank and honor my pastors Bill Johnson, senior pastor, and Kris Vallotton, senior associate pastor, Bethel Church, for paving the way for so many of us to apprehend and walk in our destiny. My participation at Bethel and attending Bethel's School of Supernatural Ministry (BSSM) has been an amazing and life changing experience with God. Echoes of influence from your sermons, teaching, books, activations and impartations are throughout this book.

Bonnie Johnson, Third Year BSSM Pastor, Women Who Love Revival, and author of *Kingdom Keys;* Thank you for leading me to access the Presence of God in a more tangible way.

Dawna DeSilva and Teresa Liebscher, Bethel Sozo, Shabar, and Transformation Center Ministries: Thank you for all you do to heal the broken hearted and proclaim liberty to the captives. I am so blessed to be part of the team.

Bethany Stroup, Bethel BSSM administration, author of *Cinderella's Complexion* (not yet released): Thank you for help with editing, cover layout, and so much encouragement.

Aaron McMahon, Bethel BSSM graduate classmate, author of *These Signs Shall Follow* and *How to Write & Publish Your Book*: Thank you for manuscript assistance, fixing all my formatting errors, thank you for the "*thank yous!*"

ℛECOMMENDATIONS

"It was refreshing to read an inner healing book which revealed that we could actually heal! In *Dancing on the Graves of Your Past*, Yvonne shows us that we are not simply 'survivors' stuck in mediocrity nor are we any longer victims helpless, powerless and afraid. If you want to become an overcomer, then you'll want to learn this dance."

Dawna De Silva,
Bethel Sozo and Transformation Center Ministries,
Bethel Church, Redding, CA

Dancing on the Graves of Your Past presents a powerful journey from understanding our trauma and wounds to courageously choosing to live as victorious overcomers in Christ. Using her life experience as a backdrop, Yvonne Martinez gives us valuable words of wisdom and profound spiritual insights that heal the damage from abuse and painful life experiences. I have heard testimonies from friends and my own clients who have benefited greatly from Yvonne's speaking and writing.

Barry Byrne, MFT (Marriage & Family Therapist)
Love After Marriage and President, Living Strong, Inc., Redding, CA

"We are all searching for wisdom and insight to those personal issues that hold us back from moving forward to fulfilling our GOD ordained destiny. Yvonne has by inspiration of the Holy Spirit presented us with exactly that and a map included. I love this book! Yvonne's insights, revelations and guidance are priceless and practical. This is a must have book for every working minister who specializes in counseling or areas of freedom and heart healing sessions. It is perfect for a group designed to dig into the rich treasury. Each individual can receive pearls of wisdom while allowing the Holy Spirit to sift their soul, bring brilliances and healing to their heart. I could not recommend anyone more highly as a teacher, counselor and author. She has the years of experience to back each word. Yvonne has opened the door for us to enter into a glorious dance with our KING. Lets all take HIS hand and be transformed into HIS beautiful and radiant children."

Rev. E. Pauline Hailstone BSW
President of Broken Alabaster Box Ministries
Founder of Lydia House Restoration Program for Women
Co-founder of Alaska prayer network
Governmental level prophetic intercessor & leader
Eagle River, Alaska

"It was my privilege to have Yvonne as my intern (2007-2008) and grew to know and love her. The victories of faith and perseverance that God has bestowed upon her are a blessing and inspiration to the body of Christ and to woman who have endured similar experiences. Her life is a manifestation of Kingdom power and promise that *"all things work together for good for those who love God and are called according to His purpose.* Romans 8:28."

Bonnie Johnson
BSSM 3rd year overseer 2001-2009
Bethel Church, Redding, CA

TABLE OF CONTENTS

Dear Reader,

Your unresolved emotional anxiety and pain no longer need to breathe down your neck or hang around your ankles, keeping you bound. The King of Kings has sent you an invitation to partner with Him in the Kingdom and dance face to face.

However, to embrace intimacy and dance face to face with the King of Kings, you will need to exchange a cloak of mourning for a robe of righteousness and abandon the grave site where your past and all your sorrows were atoned for through Jesus' death on the Cross.

Your journey of embracing Him will be marked with crossroads where important decisions will need to be made. At times you may feel unsure and afraid but God sent you His Holy Spirit, called The Comforter for a reason, to draw you into the Father's arms and trust His lead.

Dancing on the Graves of Your Past is an invitation to say "goodbye" to your past, rise to your feet and take ownership of your partnership with the living God.

Your acceptance of His invitation can move you forward into your destiny, a fulfilled life of freedom with the King, accessing and activating your inheritance in the Kingdom of God. Otherwise, you may remain bound to a familiar, painful past and, thereby, forfeit the blessings and inheritance Jesus died to give you.

The decision to say *"yes"* is in the heart of everyone who has cried out for help and I believe you, like me, have chosen to dance with the King.

I recently passed the half way point, now living as many years in freedom and victory as I once did in emotional pain. The journey is worth it.

The *dances* I share with you are keys to unlock the shackles around your ankles so you can experience authentic intimacy and the benefits of belonging to Him.

He is waiting so let's begin...

"I pray also that the eyes of your heart may be enlightened in order that you may know the hope to which he has called you, the riches of his glorious inheritance in the saints, and his incomparably great power for us who believe." — Eph. 1: 18

In His Service,
Yvonne Martinez

Yesteryears

Sad, cruel memories
of life's dark path
rehearse in your mind.
The clouds engulf you
thundering the pain
of yesterday's great fears.
Trust the Savior
living inside you
to blow away the storm.
Pick up your banner
shout new praises
the victory has been won.
The foe already
lost the war
through Calvary's crimson flow.
Don't let tears
from yesteryears
wash the Son from your life today.
Don't let the tears
from yesteryears
wash away today.

—*Yvonne Martinez*

"*In the plan of the Great Dance plans without number interlock, and each movement becomes in its season the breaking into flower of the whole design to which all else had been directed. Thus each is equally at the centre and none are there by being equals, but some by giving place and some by receiving it, the small things by their smallness and the great by their greatness, and all the patterns linked and looped together by the unions of a kneeling with a sceptred love. Blessed be He!*"

C.S. Lewis, Perelandra, excerpt from pp. 218-219

JOURNAL PAGE

Use *Journal Pages* to process,
pray or record your experience
with God as you read
*Dancing on the Graves
of Your Pas*t

Chapter 1

THE PAST

"He brought them out of darkness and the deepest
gloom and broke away their chains."
—Psalm 107:14

Paul, in Romans 8:38-39, writes, *"For I am con-*
vinced that neither death nor life, neither angels nor de-
mons, neither the present nor the future, nor any powers,
neither height nor depth, nor anything else in all creation,
will be able to separate us from the love of God that is in
Christ Jesus our Lord." Paul mentions the present and
the future, but he doesn't mention the past. The past
can't separate you from God's love because He sent
Jesus, His love incarnate, to redeem the past. But the
past *can* separate you from the awareness of God's
love.

JOURNAL PAGE

I was four years old when it happened. However, the memory of the stranger and the sexual assault was buried until adulthood. It would turn out to be the first in a long line of victimizations.

My dad was an alcoholic and spent most of my early years in prison. He had broken my mom's nose and threatened her life so we moved to Grandma's. At night he would peer into our windows and I'd hear the bushes rattle imagining an awful monster waiting to devour me. When he found out I was willing to testify against him in court, he told me, "You aren't my daughter and as far as I am concerned you don't exist."

Adolescence sent me on a search for love. My grandma tried to tell me about Jesus. I prayed on Sunday but by Monday I was sure even Jesus had forgotten me.

At 18, I married someone who was into motorcycles and parties and after our son was born he left me. Two years later I fell in love with a co-worker. We had a small wedding and weekend honeymoon. I kissed him goodbye about 9:30 on a Saturday morning. At noon, a police car pulled into the driveway. He had been in an accident and was in critical condition.

JOURNAL PAGE

As my world crumbled, I wouldn't give up hope. But hope wasn't enough. Twenty-one days later, he died. I laid my head on his chest and listened for life, but it was gone. We had been married two months and thirteen days.

Twenty-two years old with two marriages behind me, I stuffed my emotions and tried to start over. I bought a house and a business but felt lonely and afraid.

During an argument the new guy I was dating hit me hard enough to send me to the emergency room. I thought I could fix his problems so a few years later we married. He continued to be suspicious and controlling and it didn't take very long for me to realize, once again, I made another bad choice.

Waiting for a late customer, I left the door to my store unlocked while I cleaned up the back room. The bell rang alerting me someone had come into the store. Turning toward the door, a man wearing a ski mask pointed a pistol at me and said, *"Turn around or I'll blow your head off."*

I froze, knowing I couldn't outrun a bullet. He grabbed me and kept the gun pressed to my head demanding money. Covering my head with a laundry bag, he forced me onto the cement floor and

JOURNAL PAGE

raped me. The gun pressed against my temple, he said if I told anyone, he would return to kill me. When I heard the bell on the door again, I called for help.

Eventually my attacker was caught but escaped. I received threatening phone calls at my business and home. The police monitored my activities because of his threats against my life. The intensity of the crime was compounded by newspaper publicity. Customers, business associates, and friends knew. I felt ashamed and guilty, emotionally paralyzed.

A few months later my father died. I had only seen him once since that awful conversation when he disowned me but I wanted to attend the funeral. He died from alcoholism after spending years in and out of prison. My broken heart triggered when I looked inside the open casket. I realized I needed my dad to tell me he loved me. Now, he'd never be able to say the words I longed to hear. I cried for a lost relationship—for the dad I never had.

At the funeral, someone pressed a cedar box into my hands. It contained a beautiful white Bible. Looking back, the Lord was telling me, *"Little child, I will be your Father and I love you even when it seems no one else does."* I couldn't hear God then.

JOURNAL PAGE

Since the funeral was out of state and I stayed alone in a hotel, there was time to think over my life—where I had been and where I was going. My marriage had become a war of emotional games. The rape had been far more than physical. It had stolen the ability to defend myself, a rape of my soul. My father's death finalized my unworthiness. I had no hope.

The police caught the rapist again and set another trial date. He waived his right to an attorney and defended himself, which gave him access to all the evidence including my personal information.

Phone callers left threatening messages and the words after the rape resounded in my mind, *"If you tell, I'll kill you."* Overwhelming fear of leaving the house or being alone mounted as my world became smaller and smaller.

Physical problems began to surface and medical tests revealed I had cancer and five years to live. The word cancer was shocking and ugly, almost as ugly as rape. I had a hysterectomy. I was 26. Life had been unfair.

Sleep came only after exhaustion from wrestling with tormenting thoughts. I hadn't been able to stop the merry-go-round of events that held me captive. I

JOURNAL PAGE

believed I would die by the age of thirty. Thoughts of suicide dashed through my mind.

As I searched for comfort from the long terror-filled nights, a childhood song, *"Jesus loves me this I know..."* would flush away my fear. I sang the song but wondered if Jesus really could love me.

The rapist was convicted and sent to prison while the violence in my marriage escalated. The fear of remaining in the marriage became stronger than my fear of leaving. I divorced the abusive marriage and walked away from the house I owned.

Yes, you're right. I met another man. Tony was a Christian and led me to receive Jesus as my personal savior. Eighteen months later Tony and I married. Jesus was planning my life and doctors confirmed all the cancer was gone!

Joy and anticipation were easily overcome by fear and insecurity. My emotional sores were amplified when memories connected to the traumatic events surfaced and I couldn't hold back anger and tears. I still wore the old identity of my past.

I had trusted God for salvation, now I had to risk trusting Him to complete the healing I needed. Knowing He was my only hope, I purposed to press into God

JOURNAL PAGE

and allow Him to press into me. He began to heal my wounded life, not only to stop the infection but to bring me into His love and freedom. Sometimes it seemed that for every two steps forward I took one step backward. God was faithful to bring me through into the revelation and reality of his love and goodness.

Much like a recipe, you can't taste the quality of the finished product until all the ingredients are measured, mixed, and baked. As the Lord gave me the ingredients, I realized the principles were keys to a life beyond my pain, out of the darkness and into Him.

In 1984 when I first received invitations to speak and share my testimony, I asked God to reveal the process He had taken me through. With pen and paper, I wrote out my stages of growth and encounters with God.

My church hired me on Pastoral Counseling staff in 1985 where I counseled and facilitated support groups. I became a central part of a network of pastors who helped churches establish ministries reaching out to hurting people in their congregations and communities.

In 1994, my first book was released, entitled *From Victim to Victor*, (Recovery Publications). With an accompanying leader's workbook, I taught other group

JOURNAL PAGE

facilitators and my material was used in many churches and groups. Although my first book is now out of print, my growth in God didn't stop.

We saw a taste of revival throughout our ministry ventures in Alaska and it created a hunger for more of God. In 2005 we moved to Redding, CA, to be part of Bethel Church where I tucked myself into revival and graduated third year Bethel School of Supernatural Ministry. I currently serve on Bethel's Transformation Center Pastoral Counseling staff, work with Bethel Sozo teams, and co-lead *Women Who Love Revival*, a Bethel women's ministry, writing, traveling and speaking whenever I can. I continue in radical relationship with Jesus through personal relationship and outward demonstration. This year (2009) I celebrate 32 years as a Christian and 30 years married to Tony. The second half of my life has been an adventure into the fullness of the Kingdom of God. *"For he has rescued us from the dominion of darkness and brought us into the kingdom of the Son he loves..."* Col. 1:13 is a promise fulfilled!

A few years ago during Domestic Violence and Sexual Assault Awareness week, a local agency invited me to speak at their rally. They wanted a "survivor" to tell their story. I told them I wasn't a "survivor"

JOURNAL PAGE

and I didn't have a sad story. Jesus didn't die on the Cross and resurrect from the grave so I could "survive." I am saved, healed, and set-free, an overcomer called and empowered by God to bring His Kingdom to earth. I am not a victim of my past! I shared my testimony last and received a standing applause.

God partnered with us in our past when He gave us Jesus who died on the Cross and shed His Blood. Jesus took our sins and spiritual death upon Himself and through a Divine exchange, gave us complete amnesty and freedom.

When we accept Jesus' death in exchange for ours, His Cross becomes the grave site where our sin (including mistakes and bad choices) and old nature are atoned for, dead and buried, never more to be counted against us.

Then Jesus resurrected from the dead and returned to His Father in Heaven creating a bridge of reconciliation uniting Heaven and earth. Jesus now becomes the model we follow. He was a man in right relationship with God. We now have both the authority and power to be "the sons of God"... and daughters, too!

Seated with Him in Heavenly places with full access to the Kingdom's benefits, we have freedom from emotional distress, physical sickness, and spiritual torment.

JOURNAL PAGE

God partnered with us in our past so we could now partner with Him in our future.

God did it for love. He did it to destroy the works of the devil. He did it so we would be reconciled to Him. He did it so we would have a future and a hope.

JOURNAL PAGE

Chapter 2

THE INVITATION

*"But for you who revere my name, the sun of righteousness
will rise with healing in its wings. And you will go out
and leap like calves released from the stall.
Then you will trample down the wicked; they will be
ashes under the soles of your feet..."*

—Malachi 4:2-3

In the beginning I began writing letters to God, telling Him about what happened to me and telling Him how I felt. I vented and dumped all my emotions onto pieces of paper, recounting the abuse, rejection, and betrayal. I took hidden secrets out of my heart and placed them in front of God. This process brought me out of denial and led me to face the emotional pain that haunted me.

Journal Page

At that time I didn't realize from God's view my past was already forgiven and the door to the Kingdom already opened. These exercises of lamentations, graciously received by Him were, in fact, the beginning of my knowing Him. This is worth repeating...

At that time I didn't realize from God's view my past was already forgiven and the door to the Kingdom already opened. These exercises of lamentations, graciously received by Him were, in fact, the beginning of my knowing Him.

In *My Utmost for His Highest*, Oswald Chambers says that our knowing Him is like a man coming out of a dark cave into the brightness of His light. At first we can't see well, maybe even blinded by the brightness of the light, until our eyes get adjusted and we can see clearly. So it was for me. Jesus had already paid for the death and burial of my past—it was I who had to capture the revelation.

God began to slowly adjust my eyes to see Him more clearly and open my heart to accept His love. Healing came over the next three years—not all at once and not in a neat step-by-step fashion. Even though there were seasons that felt like a roller coaster ride, way up and then way down, at least I was strapped in the arms of Jesus and moving forward!

JOURNAL PAGE

Guilt and shame, rejection and betrayal tried to sing the old familiar songs of my past to keep me focused on them. Release began when I could surrender it all to Him. The biggest breakthroughs came when I realized God was listening and responding to me! His responses weren't with thunder or audible words, but I experienced pictures, songs, scripture, and assurance He was with me, bringing comfort, peace, and joy! During these moments I felt wrapped in warm blankets of His love and acceptance creating a place of rest, peace and safety.

After a time, it was no longer important what I wrote to Him, but rather what He was saying and showing me.

I began to experience more days of joy and fewer days of torment. In the distance I could hear a new sound—a song accompanied by beautiful music. He had been courting me, coaxing me onto the Kingdom's dance floor with Him as my new partner.

Surrender and forgiveness were as at the core of my prayers to God, but those were merely my exercises of letting go. I also had to be willing to embrace a new belief system about God and my relationship with Him. I learned through my own experience and from others who I have counseled, what we believe

JOURNAL PAGE

about God directly affects trusting His love and living out our destiny in Him.

He is waiting to show you the mysteries of the Kingdom, just as He did with His disciples. He is desirous of an intimate relationship with you—to hold you close to Him, closer than any human embrace. God's availability isn't the barrier. The barrier is our misconception or mistrust of Him. Barriers are dissolved when we catch the revelation of who He is.

I know some things about the President of the United States. I know where he resides, what his duties are, and when he is on an overseas tour. But if I were asked about his personal thoughts or how to contact him in an emergency I wouldn't know. Even if I read his autobiography, I would have detailed information about him, but we would not be in relationship.

The same is true with God. Simply knowing about Him isn't enough. To assume we know God's will and desire for us without really knowing Him or His nature leaves us relying on our own faulty judgment and assumptions. Allowing past circumstances to be a guide for the future is like speeding down a steep road. What creates a victim is not what has happens to

JOURNAL PAGE

us, but remaining stuck in a pattern of thinking, believing there are limited, or no, choices.

A "victim mentality" places a ceiling on options and choices. We actually exchange the truth for a lie, and stay trapped in a cycle of unsuccessful attempts to fix something broken using broken tools. Here are a few examples.

Cindy loved God and was active in her church until about a year ago when her teenage son was killed in an automobile accident. Deep down inside she believed God may have taken her son away as punishment for an abortion she had as a teenager.

Dale had been a Christian for many years but on occasion he purchased pornographic videos from an adult bookstore. He would feel guilty and ask God to heal him of his sexual struggle. After losing numerous battles with temptation, Dale believed even God couldn't, or wouldn't, help him.

A married Christian man was suspected of committing a morally degrading crime and held in a local jail. The accusation and humiliation were more than he could bear. After a few hours, the initial investigation proved his innocence but when the guards went to release him, they found he had hung himself with his belt.

49

JOURNAL PAGE

Israel made a similar mistake in believing the Lord had led them into despair. They asked, "Why is the Lord bringing us to this land only to let us fall by the sword?" (Num. 14:3). Over and over they thought that bad circumstances amounted to fatal situations.

Peter, after Jesus' crucifixion, was confronted about his association with Jesus and lied (Matt. 26:69,70). In the midst of confusion and uncertainty Peter couldn't hang onto what he had known to be true about Jesus or Jesus' teachings. Overcome by fear and doubt, Peter moved into unbelief based on his circumstances.

After Jesus' burial in the tomb Mary's heart was broken believing Jesus was gone. Grief stricken over Jesus' death, she was weeping at the tomb's entrance. Mary, focused on her grief, was unaware Jesus was behind her until He called her by name (John 20:15).

These examples teach us three valuable principles.

- As long as we can trust the Lord and wait on Him, there is opportunity to see His ability to rescue and redeem us.

- Losing the ability to make choices removes hope.

JOURNAL PAGE

- Choosing a desperate course of action often results in unfortunate experiences.

Until we learn differently, we can make the mistake of believing God is like a person we know—someone who failed to love, nourish, or accept; or someone who failed to love enough to correct and confront.

God's desire for you is greater then you can imagine or think. "*...no mind has conceived what God has prepared for those who love Him*" (1Cor.2:9). God has prepared things for us that are beyond our imagination and exceed our mental capacity. Our minds are a great creation of God, but our mind can hinder and limit our receptivity to experience the greatness of the Kingdom. We were meant to be ruled by our spirit, in-filled with His Holy Spirit. Filled with unbelief, doubt and fear, we journey through the maze of our minds to find answers, rather than into His Presence.

Jesus said if I was born again, I would be able to *see* the Kingdom (John 3:3). Jesus is talking about a revelatory experience here and now. The Kingdom is available to us, but we have to put on our "son" glasses to access it. God wants you to have full access to the benefits Jesus died for—that includes you getting your

JOURNAL PAGE

full Kingdom inheritance, the "life more abundantly" talked about in John 10:10.

My pastor, Bill Johnson, says what you think you know will hold you back from what you need to know unless you remain a novice. The biggest challenge we face is to remain open to *"all things are possible with God"* (Matt: 19:26).

Your false beliefs about God are corrected in intimate relationship with Him, allowing the ceiling of limitation and expectation to be replaced with anticipation and expectancy.

Making a choice to partner with God in your destiny is walking in identification with Jesus, rather than identification with your current circumstances, what has happened to you or the mistakes you made. What happens around you or to you isn't who you are and it doesn't define who you are called to be.

Lies we believe create the battles we fight. Fear creates a lifestyle that encircles around the lies and doesn't confront the truth until you face it. Hurt causes you to close your heart. The same wall that holds out pain also holds out love. When you choose to love it pushes you past the pain.

JOURNAL PAGE

Mary tuned away from the grave site where grief and loss consumed her and turned to face Jesus. We must turn away from whatever is keeping us from looking at Him. This means we have to identify and acknowledge the things we have been giving our attention to, the things we have been clinging and holding onto—the dances we danced when we were hurting.

The King of Kings, Jesus, is inviting you to dance with Him in the Kingdom. If we will dance with Him, He will enter our pain and lead us out. The invitation set before us is to turn our attention and focus toward Him.

JOURNAL PAGE

Chapter 3

OLD MUSIC

*"The dead man came out, his hands and feet wrapped
with strips of linen, and a cloth around his face. Jesus
said to them, Take off the grave clothes and let him go."*
—John 11:44

As a pastoral counselor I meet with people who are experiencing some variation of personal conflict resulting from spiritual, emotional, physical, and/or sexual issues. Unresolved conflicts became personal cancers that ate away at their hope and sabotaged their future.

Most of us are born with the belief we are safe. However, when abuse occurs, trust and safety is breached. Intrusion through trust and safety can be a traumatic emotional disturbance and continued emotional disruption. Trauma is often experienced as a

JOURNAL PAGE

forced exposure interrupting and penetrating a safe environment.

Like the music playing in the background during a movie, the memories experienced with trauma and associated feelings create a backdrop from which life is lived and choices are made. The Old Music is the trumpeting of residual pain.

Post traumatic reactions may include anxiety, terror, guilt, blaming, detachment, agitation or irritability, restlessness, loss of interest in usual activities, loss of emotional control, grief, depression, uncertainty, thoughts of suicide, withdrawal from family or friends, communication changes, "startle" reflex, sleep disturbance, change in sexual interest or function, inability to be alone, self-harm, mistrust of environment or people, changes in appetite, and sometimes obsessive or addictive behavior.

While most people just want to forget what happened and move on, they can't stop the memories from resounding in the background. Sometimes the memories are loud and penetrating and other times can be quieted or ignored. Intense focus on silencing the memories from the trauma creates an attachment. The attachment involves such focus and interaction with the symptoms that the process resembles a type

JOURNAL PAGE

of interactive *dance*. The dance is a partnership. The trauma leads and the person follows.

The dance is in unison with the rhythm of the Old Music. Attempts to decrease, ignore, fight or deny the disabling symptoms associated with the trauma actually strengthen them. Fighting against the symptoms turns focus toward them and empowers their existence—the Old Music playing louder and louder until it is all that can be heard.

The relationship dance with the Old Music enhances the survivor's ability to stay connected with the past, allowing the memory to remain alive. Rehearsing and replaying the music are attempts to try to figure out if it really happened, why it happened, how they could have stopped it or done something different, or to find ways of revenge against their abuser.

Keeping alive the memory of the trauma allows the person to re-enter the scenario in an attempt to find resolve. It helps people who are hurting to prove the validity of what happened. The victim is often the only witness of the trauma who can testify to the trauma's reality. The symptoms are proof, to themselves and others, the trauma was real. They feel that without displaying their symptoms they won't be believed.

JOURNAL PAGE

Someone may have accepted Christ as his or her Savior but still remains emotionally bonded to past trauma. His or her ears hear the truth that Jesus set them free but the awakened spiritual reality only accentuates the distance between the His truth and the Old Music. Feelings, emotions, and symptoms still attached to the Old Music are in direct conflict with the truth of God's Word.

It happens when we acknowledge the benefits of the Cross without really appropriating the Cross' benefits. The conflict surfaces because we never really allow (permit) the Cross to wash away the circumstances that draw the pain toward us. Because we hold onto our symptoms and are still in relationship with the Old Music, we respond when the memories are triggered and up they pop, painfully fresh and alive.

Sadly, we know the Old Music doesn't comfort us. It is just uncomfortably familiar, yet we keep the memory tight in our grasp. With the Old Music playing in the background, we dance the dance of guilt and shame, fear and blame, rehearsing the steps we know so well. We exchange the truth for a lie, submitting to the lie, allowing it to dominate and control us. The power of the Old Music is protected by our

JOURNAL PAGE

agreement and permission for it to remain in tact. The dance with the past is both unholy and ungodly.

Once we begin studying the Bible, we learn His Word is both a lens and a mirror. A lens magnifies the depth and revelatory mysteries of God. A mirror reflects back to us where we need to change our beliefs and mindsets in order to come into agreement and access His revelation. In other words, when we are confronted with the truth about God, we are also confronted with the truth about ourselves.

In the Psalms, David continually cries out and expresses his feelings, both happy and sad, to God. We, too, can express ourselves to Him. Feelings aren't right or wrong. They are a barometer that gauges our emotional state. One of God's gifts to us is the ability to laugh and feel joy as well as to cry and feel sadness. Our feelings are meant to work for us as an indicator of how we're doing. When our gauge begins signaling "alert... ouch... painful memory... shame... rejection" we sometimes put a pillow over the alarm.

Problems become intensified when we detach our feelings from events. This is called *denial*. Jesus was the master of confronting denial and bringing peoples issues to the surface. He didn't people please others and sometimes wasn't very nice! He stood in a posture as to

JOURNAL PAGE

allow the person to see their stuff and confronted in love.

In the story of the Samaritan woman in the Gospel of John (John 4:1-26), the Samaritan woman is going about her day and has not a clue what is about to happen. In the midst of her conversation with Jesus, He brings to the forefront her compromised past.

She has been married five times and was now living with another man. Jesus brought her emotionally painful situation right up front so she could be healed and set free. When Jesus finished talking with her, she was so happy she ran back to the village leaving her water pot behind. In confronting her pain, she was emotionally healed, filled with joy, and she left behind her old identity. She was the first evangelist in Samaria!

Sometimes a surface problem like a curtain conceals deeper, more significant issues. This happened to a woman attending a divorce recovery group. While discussing her failing marriage, she realized an even deeper struggle with rejection and betrayal from a childhood trauma involving her alcoholic father.

The benefits of allowing our past and pain to be atoned for through and buried at the Cross is in striking opposition to the consequences of burying it on our own

JOURNAL PAGE

through denial. The appropriation of the Cross, heals, cleanses and redeems. When we bury the pain on our own or try to forget about it, the volume of the Old Music may be low or muted, but it is very much alive. Because we are still in relationship with the Old Music, when the pain is triggered the emotions surface and the volume intensifies. The cycle gets reinforced, the symptoms are in control, and the Old Music has us captivated.

Why do the actions from who hurt you hold so much power over you? The Old Music has the ability to make us feel guilt or shame for what someone else did to us. I know it sounds silly, that someone would hurt you and you feel it is your fault. But it is possible to assume responsibility for the behaviors of others thereby agreeing with statements like, "It must have been my fault." Believing it was your fault is a type of false power—that you had the power to make someone behave a certain way.

You may discover that you are holding yourself responsible for the actions of others. Assuming responsibility for the sins of others can cause, what I call, "false guilt." No matter how hard you try, you cannot get rid of the guilt through repentance for these sins. They aren't yours.

JOURNAL PAGE

Failed attempts to bring closure keep the bond to the trauma cycle turning, adding more steps of shame and guilt to the dance. False guilt is relieved when we come out of agreement and refuse to carry the responsibility for something God doesn't hold us accountable for. Our agreement with the lie that it is, or was, our responsibility or our fault keeps the memory empowered and the volume of the Old Music turned up loud.

If you experience unresolved shame and guilt, ask the Lord to show you, if in any way, you contributed to your painful experience. The answer may be yes, you did, or no, you didn't. Honesty with yourself is essential. What you believe to be true will expose the stronghold empowering the Old Music. Once the question of responsibility is answered, shame and guilt can be dealt with.

This seems like a simple thing to do, of course. But many people just aren't sure how to identify responsibility. Somewhere along the line, they believed—either through assumption or accusation—they were responsible for what someone said or did.

Ruth was molested by her brother. She told a friend who promptly said, "Well, my brother tried that stuff and I told him *no*." Ruth felt guilty because

JOURNAL PAGE

she didn't tell her brother to stop. She believed it was her fault he molested her. She rehearsed the memory over and over trying to figure out why she didn't tell her brother "*no.*"

Bob frequently yelled and sometimes hit his wife when she failed to keep the house clean to his standards. His wife believed that if she could only do things better, Bob would be happy with her and stop getting angry. When the abuse continued, she blamed herself for failing to be a good wife.

Susan frequently took a shortcut home from school even though her parents insisted she take a safer, alternate route. With anguish in her voice, she told me it was her fault she was attacked and raped by two older boys because she did not follow her parents' instructions. Susan was consumed with guilt and shame.

In the 1980's when I told a pastor that I had been raped, he tipped his glasses, nodded his head, and said, "*Oh.*" A few Sundays later his sermon included his opinion on how women "ask" to be raped. His position of authority increased my shame and guilt. Because he was a pastor and an authority figure to me, his words contributed to the lie I believed about myself.

JOURNAL PAGE

To correctly answer the question of responsibility in these and our own situations, we need to have an understanding of abuse and its effects.

Here is a list of basic human needs:

- Survival (food, shelter, clothing)
- Safety (physical, emotional)
- Touching, skin contact
- Attention
- Mirroring and echoing
- Guidance
- Listening
- Participating
- Acceptance
- Opportunity to grieve losses and to grow
- Support
- Loyalty and trust
- Accomplishment
- Sexuality
- Enjoyment or fun
- Freedom
- Nurturing
- Unconditional love, including connection with God

JOURNAL PAGE

Abuse is the exploitation or neglect of basic human needs. It can be defined as wrongful, unreasonable, or harmful treatment by word or deed. A child who is trapped in an abusive situation is like a prisoner of war with no power, no leverage, and no voice. Abuse has many faces.

Emotional Abuse

Words are powerful. The writer of Proverbs 15:4 says, *"The tongue that brings healing is a tree of life, but a deceitful tongue crushes the spirit."*

Emotional abuse demeans a person's character and dignity and assaults self-esteem. *"Sticks and stones may break my bones, but names will never hurt me"* just isn't true. A child's world can be built by words of encouragement and acceptance or destroyed by cruel, demeaning words. Neglect—the absence of words, time, or touch—leaves a child emotionally hungry, literally starved for attention.

With tears in his eyes, Robert told me his father had never hugged him or said the words, *"I love you."* Unfortunately, many children like Robert grow up never knowing if they are wanted or loved simply because they aren't told.

JOURNAL PAGE

Types of emotional abuse include name calling, criticism, unrealistic expectations, absence of affection, not seeing the person's heart, not listening or affirming, belittling, blaming, and embarrassment.

Physical Abuse

Physical abuse results in bruises, black eyes, and broken bones; sometimes even death. Every blow causes damage to a person's dignity.

Punishing (inflicting harm through anger), rather than disciplining (training to bring about correction), is abusive treatment. The child is left confused, unable to understand the parent's action.

Physical abuse can range from withholding meals or other necessities of life to violent and unpredictable outbursts.

Women who admit being slapped or punched have said the humiliation and degradation out weighed the physical pain. The cycle of domestic violence affects children caught between two people they love. Children raised in physically abusive homes learn to inflict harm on others as a way to control people and situations.

JOURNAL PAGE

Sexual Abuse

Sexual abuse among adults consists of any sexual activity against a person's will. It can involve viewing or touching for the purpose of sexual stimulation.

Sexual abuse of a child by an adult consists of sexual activity for the purpose of adult sexual stimulation.

Many children perpetuate sexual abuse toward other children as a result of his or her experience with being sexually abused. Sexual abuse of a child opens up sexual awareness much before God's intended time. Children are left confused and often unable to negotiate the effect of the interaction.

Children who have been sexually abused are damaged emotionally and often report feelings of worthlessness, betrayal, and helplessness. Sexually abused children tend to make poor choices regarding relationships and have trouble with intimacy, especially in marriage.

Types of sexual abuse can also include pornography, the exposing of sexual activity, lusting after someone, telling sexually explicit jokes, ridiculing parts of the body, misinforming about sexual function as well as violent and predatory behavior.

JOURNAL PAGE

Randy was sexually abused by his uncle who was also his Sunday school teacher.

Questions and confusion about God are sometimes difficult to resolve when trust has been violated by an adult, such as a parent, uncle, teacher, or pastor, who held positions of spiritual authority.

Here are a few misconceptions about abuse.

Abuse Should Be Minimized

"I guess I should be grateful it wasn't worse. This has happened to lots of people." I hear that statement quite a bit from my counseling clients. In reality, abuse damages a person irrespective of duration, who the offender was, or the level of interaction. I like what Larry Crabb, a professional counselor and author, said during one of his seminars…*"The size of the gun doesn't determine if you have been shot."*

Abuse Heals with Time

"It has been five years. Why should I have to go through this again? I don't want to discuss it." However, time is not a healer—only a distancer from the pain.

JOURNAL PAGE

Abuse Can Be Defined by the Act

"He never actually touched me, but I hated the way he looked at my body. I feel so stupid because I can't describe what he did." A person is abused when they are deprived of basic human needs or when their dignity is diminished or exploited.

It is unfair to the victim to imply a label be given to the event before feelings can be validated. The lack of validation or concern from others perpetuates the victim's need to hang onto the memory causing them to further express symptoms in an effort to be believed. But when pain is denied a type of emotional anorexia can develop to protect the victim from any feelings at all. Depression medications often suppress anxiety and stress but can also level out joy and creativity causing life to stagnate.

Secrets are sickness but openness is wholeness. Keeping a secret is very powerful. As long as the secret stays hidden, you hold onto a false sense of power that keeps you in control.

You may be wondering about the necessity to confront someone who hurt you. Confrontation isn't a prerequisite for healing. My father died before I was

JOURNAL PAGE

a Christian and began to deal with my pain. Therefore, I couldn't confront him directly. However, I could confront the truth.

Confrontation is about courage and love and the willingness to discuss conflict. But it should be done from a place of strength. Unless the offender recognizes and accepts his or her responsibility, you will set yourself up for more rejection and hurt. If you are still in danger of being hurt, you should refrain from that relationship until you and, hopefully, the offender can get some help.

JOURNAL PAGE

Chapter 4

OLD DANCES

"Surely you desire truth in the inner parts; you teach me wisdom in the inmost place. Cleanse me with hyssop, and I will be clean; wash me, and I will be whiter than snow. Let me hear joy and gladness; let the bones you have crushed rejoice. Hide your face from my sins and blot out all my iniquity. Create in me a pure heart, O God, and renew a steadfast spirit within me. Do not cast me from your presence or take your Holy Spirit from me. Restore to me the joy of your salvation and grant me a willing spirit, to sustain me. "
—Psalm 51:6-12

Adam and Eve were created to rule in dominion. Yet, in the midst of their most perfect environment, Eve contemplated there could be something she was

JOURNAL PAGE

lacking. The voice of doubt serenaded her with lyrics that followed an enchanting melody. She embraced it as her own and through one encounter of agreement, she was dancing with the enemy, swaying to and fro, listening to lyrics that soothed her soul (Gen.1).

Once the truth was recognized the dance of deception ended but the dance of shame and guilt began. Adam and Eve tried to cover their wrong actions by hiding from God. Guilt and shame were the result of real actions and choices. Looking at their life from our vantage point, it is easy to trace the steps and recognize where they messed up then tried to cover it up.

Yes, Eve's enemy deceived her. However Eve became the victim of deception at the point of agreement with the lies of the enemy. The music of intrigue and deception orchestrated by the enemy quickly became a dance of shame and guilt. The Old Dances are the coping mechanisms we use to cover the shame and guilt from our actions and choices.

The Old Dances of guilt and shame are sustained by the lyrics, melodies, and chorus changes (Old Music) we knew by heart. The Old Dance chooses distance rather than relationship. Distance (fear and hiding) enables us to remain in control.

JOURNAL PAGE

God sent Jesus to redeem us from the Old Dance of guilt and shame, messing up and covering up. We have the opportunity to rule in dominion through the power of the resurrected Jesus. This is the Dance of the Kingdom in the arms of the One who knows us best and loves us the most. Jesus' power of the Cross, His Blood, His Atonement, and His Resurrection made it possible.

Jesus didn't die *for* us, He died *as* us, so our sins would no longer be connected or attributed to us (2 Cor. 5:21). His Cross is where the funeral occurred. Our old nature, our sins, our mistakes and our bad choices are all accounted for and discharged at the Cross, the place of our atonement and thereby the grave site of all our sin. Paul does an excellent job of explaining this to us in Romans 6—the death of Christ wipes out, cancels, and obliterates the record of our old nature.

A grave is a burial place, a place of internment, a final resting place, or the end of something. Dead things are buried in graves. Necromancy is having a relationship with something that is dead. As gross as that sounds, it is what we do when we remain in relation with the past and allow the past to control our future.

JOURNAL PAGE

It happens very subtly. The Old Music gets louder and louder until it has gained our full attention. And then, here we go, with picks and shovels, the pain resurrected and resuscitated. With deception revived, the Old Dance of coping is all too familiar. After all, we already know the steps. It is the same old lie that enticed Eve, lyrics rearranged to personally minister to our longing and need.

The more uncomfortable process of the Holy Spirit reveals our connection to the Old Dances, our hurtful actions and attitudes toward others. It is God's answer to our prayer from Psalm 51:6-12 to *"create in me a pure heart."*

As children, we often needed self-protection to survive deprivation, neglect, or violence. As adults, our learned ways of protection can become the walls that close us in and keep everyone else out. Walls of self-protection become the obstacles that block intimate relationships.

My friends, Norma and Steve, adopted a newborn girl, Natalie, who was seriously ill. As an infant, her illness required twenty-four hour care. Either mom or dad was with her at all times. After she had outgrown the medical problems, her parents were able to leave her with a reliable babysitter. However, it seemed the

JOURNAL PAGE

only way Natalie could cope with the absence of her parents was to hide in her bed, cover herself with blankets and go to sleep. Today, at ten years old, she still displays fear of being abandoned and is very un-cooperative and sometimes rude toward others.

As a young toddler if Rick cried after being put to bed, one of his parents would come in his room and violently shake the bed. This method stopped Rick from crying but also paralyzed him with fear at the sudden impact of his body flying up and down on the shaking bed in a dark room. Rick grew up with a fear of speaking out and expressing his needs. Conse-quently, he has never been able to trust close relation-ships or move beyond superficial conversations.

Children learn methods to protect themselves when they feel insecure or threatened. Both Natalie and Rick are coping with childhood events (the Old Music) that weren't within their power to control. However, they both compensated with behaviors that sheltered their pain (Old Dances) to help them deal with life. They adopted methods of self-protection to keep them safe.

Self-protective patterns can become the broken glasses through which life is viewed. Adults living with residual pain (Old Music) and recurring coping patterns

Journal Page

(Old Dances) become imprisoned. The patterns that once protected now keep us locked up and the adult heart flutters and fights against the bars for freedom, thus the dances are in full swing.

Adults who live their lives through a coping mechanism or from a defensive position repeat patterns in choices and select, by default, the same unfulfilling reactions. They choose and make future decisions based on underlying false beliefs. The coping behavior is a vehicle to keep the pain shielded, like a bandage covering an open wound.

Initially the bad events may have happened to you without your choice involved. If the belief of helplessness takes hold you may expect someone, or God, to do something *to* you, or *for* you, to make it right or fix it. *"I am powerless and things only happen to me."* This belief keeps you stuck and cripples the ability to take ownership of choices or take steps to change. Walls are often reinforced with self-pity. Self-pity strategically accesses guilt and shame through the pain of the Old Music.

In contrast there can be a sense of entitlement. Since all these bad things happened to me...*I am entitled to compensation, free counseling, unending attention*

JOURNAL PAGE

from others. I am entitled to mistreat others, be angry, and take out my pain on you.

Sonia is an adult woman with 4 children. Sonia's mother whines and manipulates Sonia to get her needs met. After Sonia complies, mom criticizes Sonia for every action not approved of. Sonia has been trapped in her mother's control since a young girl. Sonia is frustrated and angry, feeling she can never please her mom. She is filled with self-contempt; yet, Sonia never thought she had the ability or power to set boundaries and limits. Somehow, this would dishonor her mom. Sonia, on the other hand, is mean and abrupt with her husband and children. She doesn't see that she is taking out her pain and anger on the people she loves the most.

Feelings of rejection, betrayal, hatred, anger, unforgiveness, and ambivalence are natural responses to being hurt. But when we harbor and protect them, we often reshape them into weapons to hurt ourselves or someone else. The coping mechanism or protective attitude reveals itself through sinful behaviors, manipulation and compromised actions.

Reacting out of our pain causes us to sin against others and God. By justifying our sin, we excuse or deny the thoughts and behaviors that hurt others. We

JOURNAL PAGE

may say, *"This is just how I am,"* or *"I've always been like this, and that is just how it is."* Or *"You have no idea what I have been through."* Justifying our actions is an invitation and excuse to rebel. Finally, we discount true guilt, God's conviction for our sin, and deny Jesus' atoning work on the Cross.

When God begins the work of showing us our defenses and protective behaviors, He also identifies attitudes we were completely unaware we carried. The Holy Spirit, called the Comforter or Counselor (John 14), brings the truth and inward cleansing and the changing necessary *"to be conformed to the likeness of his Son"* (Rom. 8:29). God instructs us not to partner with darkness rather to let darkness be exposed (Eph 5:11). It is His love for us that drags what is in darkness into the light. Healing requires we remain humble and honest and allow the deep work when the Holy Spirit draws our attention to the underlying issues and the ways we have created unholy and ungodly bonding.

Sinful cycles pass down from generation to generation. (Look up Exodus 34:7 and Numbers 14:18.) We can experience God's forgiveness and restoration through Jesus by repenting (turning away from) and renouncing our sinful thoughts and behavior.

JOURNAL PAGE

According to 2 Cor. 5:21, "*God made him who had no sin to be sin for us, so that in him we might become the righteousness of God.*" And Psalm 112:2 gives us a promise that the generations of the upright—the righteous—will be blessed!

When we invite the work of the Holy Spirit, He brings us into all truth. The Old Music and Old Dances have no power, control, influence, or dominance when demolished and disempowered through Jesus. True peace comes from being cleansed by God's grace and forgiveness.

JOURNAL PAGE

Chapter 5

DANCE OF SURRENDER

I will both lie down in peace, and sleep, for
you alone, O LORD, make me dwell in safety.
— Psalm 4:8

Jesus danced the Dance of Surrender so He and His Father would be "One." It was the beginning of Jesus following His Father's direction so in all ways He would be submitted to His Father. The Dance of Surrender is coming out of yourself and into God. It is about trusting Him—allowing Him to lead us into true freedom and peace.

As a child dances on the feet of their father so begins our Dance of Surrender. Our Heavenly Father

JOURNAL PAGE

knows our heart. He moves slowly and holds us close so we don't fall. Our first dance with Him beautifully demonstrates our "oneness" with Him as we move intimately together.

At the close of many church meetings, the preacher petitions the congregation with Jesus' invitation, *"'Come unto me, all you who are weary and burdened, and I will give you rest. Take my yoke upon you and learn from me, for I am gentle and humble in heart, and you will find rest for your souls'"* (Matt. 11:28, 29). The preacher then asks, *"Won't you come to the altar and give it to Jesus?"* The people march forward, pray a few moments, and go home to find they took "it" with them.

This reminds me of when my toddlers placed inedible and undesirable things in their mouths. We called it "yuck." I'd coax, *"Give mommy the yuck,"* requesting dirt, coins, bugs, or whatever, to be spit out of their mouth and into the palm of my hand. If the yuck came out, I'd applaud and praise with a sigh of relief. If the yuck had been swallowed no matter how much I coaxed or commanded, a voluntary spit wasn't going to expel the yuck. The only way the bad stuff was going to come out was by emptying the stomach.

JOURNAL PAGE

Giving our problems to Jesus is similar. A simple word or two usually won't do it. It requires an emptying of self-will and self-protection. The "coming" must be accompanied with sincere motivation and desire to be rid of our "yuck." Resistance to surrender will drive us to the edge and limit of our own strength.

What does the Old Music and Old Dance offer that generates resistance to surrender? The answers are in the completion of the following statement;

If I keep this trauma-bond relationship in tact I won't have to feel, have an identity, face others, be responsible, be authentic, change, tell secrets, be honest, tell my truth, trust, be in reality, be positive, grow, be accountable, have relationships, be mature, risk, have goals, have values, be independent, have freedom, have internal validation, have a purpose, be connected with people or family, have dreams, have hopes, be successful, have faith, live, be in the present, obtain status, make decisions, have needs, have wants, have communication, intimacy with God or...(insert as it applies)

Resistance causes us to pray to relieve the symptoms rather than pray for revelation so there won't be symptoms. Sometimes it is easier to keep cleaning up the messes than to find out why we keep making them

JOURNAL PAGE

Lasting change happens when we change our belief system rather than our behavior system.

The systems of the Old Music and Old Dance perpetuate fear of facing the future. Surrender is risk and willingness to face the future through faith and exercising trust through relationship with God.

The process can expose and trigger pain of vulnerability as that which we first experienced during the original trauma. Remember, when I was talking about trauma being a forced intrusion into a safe environment? The person in protective mode perceives themselves as now being safe. Protection is a disguise. Any intrusion into that artificially safe place is felt as penetrating and painful.

Alice was the youngest of three sisters, all of whom were molested by their stepfather. The problem today is that her mother is old and in poor health. Alice is going to visit her and wants to try to work things out, but there is something blocking her.

As a child, Alice believed her mother knew about the molestation and was not capable, or unable, to protect her so Alice made herself a secret promise. She made an internal vow she would never trust her mother again. Since that time and throughout Alice's adult years, Alice and her mom have never had more

JOURNAL PAGE

than a superficial connection. She knows she must let go of the vow of mistrust so she can forgive, heal, and make an attempt to build relationship with her mother.

Jessica was undisciplined and disruptive in her Sunday school class. The teacher was determined to take control of her class and Jessica! So with patience, kindness, goodness, and gentleness she gave Jessica lots of special attention.

Jessica was hugged, talked to, and finally the teacher pulled her up onto the teacher's lap. When the teacher reached to tickle her just above the knee, Jessica suddenly pushed the teacher's hand away and abruptly pulled her dress down over her knees. With a confident tone of voice, Jessica said, *"My uncle touched my private and he is in jail and I never have to see him again."* With that statement, Jessica jumped out of the teacher's lap and began her usual disruptive activities.

Jessica, at age five, had made a promise to herself that no one would control her again. As an adult, Jessica's commitment to that promise still holds her bound.

The dances of self-protection Alice and Jessica learned in childhood are affecting their relationships

JOURNAL PAGE

with others. Resistance to intimacy is fortified by promises we made to the Old Music and Old Dances. Today, if we want to grow in our relationships, we can no longer afford to keep these promises. Jesus wants our stability, security, and significance to be in Him.

The path to true happiness and peace is to love God with our whole heart, mind, soul, and strength.

David writes in Psalm 51:18, *"The sacrifices of God are a broken spirit; a broken and contrite heart, O God, you will not despise."* David responded so openly and truthfully after failing at his own strong-willed attempts to remedy his denial and deceitfulness. We may call Jesus our *Savior* but not allow him Lordship over our lives. Without surrender the Old Music and Old Dance have an open invitation for relationship with the lies that empower shame, guilt, and fear.

Thomas, in John, Chapter 14, was concerned after hearing Jesus' plans to go away. Thomas questioned Jesus and His promise He would not leave them, but would return to them. Jesus tells Thomas and the disciples *"I will not leave you as orphans...."* Jesus discerned Thomas' insecurity and fear. In recognition of Thomas attitude, Jesus identifies an "orphan" spirit manifested in Thomas' fear of being left alone, unprotected, uncovered, rejected and abandoned.

JOURNAL PAGE

Jesus promised He wouldn't leave them as orphans but will send them the Holy Spirit called the Spirit of Truth (John 14:17) also translated in Greek as "The Comforter." Jesus also called the Holy Spirit "The Counselor" in John 14:26. In other words, Jesus was sending them Truth, Comfort, and Counsel in the form of the Holy Spirit. who would be both *with* and *inside* them.

The orphan spirit, in an attempt to hide pain and brokenness, seeks protection and cover up from allies. Three prominent allies are the *unloving spirit*, the *religious spirit* and the *punishing spirit*. If these barriers exist, they must be conquered so surrender will be pure and unhindered, or manipulated.

The Unloving Spirit

During a support group a young woman remained reserved and distant. We encouraged her to let God have her pain. *"I don't like to pray out loud,"* she said. We said we would join her in silent prayer. She refused. We encouraged her to tag along on our prayers. She refused. Perplexed and trying to build a bridge through her resistance, I offered her, once more, to allow us to pray for her. Now crying, she

JOURNAL PAGE

shook her head and firmly refused. She was unable to receive God's love and forgiveness.

The unloving spirit protects the orphaned heart by blocking the ability to give and receive love both from others and God. The melody plays in harmony with the Old Music, rooted in the past and its footsteps can be tracked throughout the Old Dances. Out of default, the unloving spirit will reject before it gets rejected— it will desire love but behave unlovely.

Love actually brings justice and requires protection. Those who are unable to give and receive love reject the work of the Cross and the Blood of Jesus and thereby reject the "love" God sent them.

The unloving spirit manipulates the orphan heart with unworthiness, pity, condemnation, and accusation. It judges, accuses, criticizes and manipulates. It will embrace the comfortably uncomfortable, rather than surrender to God's love.

Because the Old Music and Old Dance maneuver a perpetual state of need, longing for love, always on the brink of crisis, the orphaned heart ends up asking what more God could possibly want them to do. And that is their problem. God doesn't want them to do anything. He wants them to let Him do something! He

JOURNAL PAGE

wants them to allow His love and infilling so they experience love and can love others.

The invalid man by the pool of Bethesda in John's Gospel (John 5:8) had been a victim of his circumstance for so long that when Jesus asked him if he wanted to be well, he began rehearsing his problem. Jesus already knew the problem. All the man needed to do was to come out of focus on himself and come into focus on God.

Jesus then commanded the invalid to pick up his mat and walk. The man picked up his mat and walked. He was cured! Later, when Jesus found the man, he told him, *"... you are well again. Stop sinning or something worse may happen to you"* (John 5:14). The reference to the man's sin raised a question for me. What sin was Jesus referring to? Jesus' comment was caution against any temptation to live his life separated from love. Jesus was warning him not to follow after an unloving spirit. Now that Jesus had healed him, a greater dimension of relationship was expected. Jesus considered anything less than that to be a sin. Many people are camped out by their own pools of despair and Jesus' invitation to surrender will evoke excuses, an inability to receive love.

JOURNAL PAGE

The Religious Spirit

The religious spirit covers the orphaned heart with performance and works. Completing a fifteen-week self-defense course, their lives in neat little packages, and along comes the "invitation" to give it all up! *"You must be kidding! I have worked very hard to get where I am and no one is going to take it from me again. Only the strong survive."*

The orphaned heart's pain is covered by masks of overeating, oversleeping, overworking, or addictions to pornography, alcohol, drugs, or self-injury. Sometimes the religious spirit is manifested in fear, hiding the orphan heart behind locks, security buildings, police dogs, whistles, or self-defense classes; maybe hiding behind anger, verbal abuse, assault, pride, procrastination and even hopelessness.

Consequently, the religious spirit is fixated on self-reliance and those things which they can control. Within the Old Music and Old Dance they have created a fortress and any uninvited intrusion reinforces the barriers.

Mark's Gospel story about a rich young man gives us another illustration. *"Jesus looked at him and loved him. ... 'Go, sell everything you have and give to the poor,*

Journal Page

and you will have treasure in heaven. Then come, follow me.' At this the man's face fell. He went away sad, because he had great wealth" (Mark 10:21-23). Jesus' concern wasn't the man's wealth, but the man's heart, which placed wealth above his relationship with Jesus. Just like this rich man, the religious spirit will hang onto any thing they believe they need more than they need Jesus.

Surrender to the Lord requires being real. Oswald Chambers says in My Utmost for His Highest says to every degree in which we are not real, we will dispute rather than come to Jesus. When someone runs to anything or anyone but Jesus, their actions indicate they don't trust him. And if they aren't trusting in Him, they are trusting in something else.

New Testament examples of the Pharisees and their relationship to God reveal attitudes and actions that were religious and resistant to God. They thought they had all the answers and missed the only true answer—Jesus. We can learn from them about the fruitlessness of a braced, unreachable heart.

Principles that hold higher value than relationship create form without purpose and tradition without power. The religious spirit is self-imposed control.

JOURNAL PAGE

Punishing Spirit

The punishing spirit denies the work of the Cross, the Blood of Jesus and the Resurrection as payment for our sin and mistakes. It blocks from receiving amnesty and forgiveness demanding greater payment. Continuing to punish ourselves for the reasons Christ died for us leads to self-destruction. The punishing spirit strikes with a whip entitled "regret," strategically mutilating hope, confidence and encouragement. It rises in contest to the power of Jesus' Blood.

The punishing spirit gateways to *"hope deferred that makes the heart sick"* (Prov.13:12) rather than hope in the finished work of the Cross (Heb. 6:19).

Jesus asks the orphan heart to, *"Come unto me."* The unloving spirit says, *"I can't,"* the religious spirit says, *"I won't,"* the punishing spirit says *"I don't deserve it."*

The antidote for the orphan spirit is experiencing the Holy Spirit. The Holy Spirit also brings the Spirit of Adoption to encircle and fill the orphan heart, calling to surrender to the *"Daddy"* relationship so desperately needed. *"For you did not receive a spirit that makes you a slave again to fear, but you have received*

JOURNAL PAGE

the Spirit of sonship. And by him we cry, Abba Father. The Spirit himself testifies with our spirit that we are God's children." (Romans 8:15,16)

I was sharing with someone about Lazarus (John 11:38-43 being raised from the dead and Jesus instructing the people to remove the old grave clothes. I told them Jesus gives us new life in Him and clothes us in a new identity. She looked down and with tears welled up in her eyes, she said, "*That is frightening to me. If all the old clothes are gone, who will I be?*"

Luke 19 tells of a parable of ten men each given a mina (about 3 months wages) to invest. All but one invests and receives a profit. The one buried the gift out of fear. He placed the gift where he was more comfortable—at the grave. When you are more comfortable at the gravesite than in the Kingdom, you will bury your blessings rather than let them multiply and prosper.

We cannot truly surrender with hands grasping the grave's head stone. We must surrender with hands grasping the Kingdom. Through conflict and pain we can enter the Kingdom and apprehend it. Eph. 5:14 tells us, "*Awake, O sleeper, and rise from the dead, the light shine in your heart to reveal the Kingdom.*"

JOURNAL PAGE

Dance of Surrender

Personally, putting all my trust into Jesus was not nearly as frightening as spending the rest of my life being chased by fear, guilt and shame. My hour of desperation motivated me and I *came to Him*, forgiving and renouncing (coming out of agreement) with all the pledges and vows I made to past emotional, physical, and traumatic relationships. I entered the Dance of Surrender where my heart was vulnerable and God carried me in His arms.

The experience of trusting Him enables me to access His Presence any time. I continue to allow Him to hold me, protect me, and instruct me because now I'm free to let Him love me. David said it so sweetly in Psalm 34:8, *"Taste and see that the Lord is good; blessed is the man who takes refuge in him."*

F – forsaking
A – all
I – I
T – take
H – Him

I once saw a cartoon that adds an illustration. A perplexed and bewildered man stands at the altar for prayer. On one side is an evangelist praying, *"God,*

JOURNAL PAGE

help him to let go ... Oh God, help him to let go." But on the man's other side is different evangelist praying, "*Oh God, help him to hang on ... Oh God, help him to hang on.*"

The Dance of Surrender is the loving process whereby we willingly let go of the Old Music and Old Dances while being romanced in the arms of Jesus into Kingdom reality. We let go while we hang on!

Surrender is an opportunity to deal with pain in a different way. How we deal with pain is a lesson in dealing with evil. Rather than looking for an escape it requires actually holding onto the pain long enough to take it to God.

Loss positions you for justice and transparency unleashes breakthrough. The perils and tribulations of living in a fallen world give us an opportunity to press into His Presence.

When we surrender to God, He always gives us something better in exchange. God always trades up! Isaiah 61:3 gives us an example of God's exchange system.

- He gives us a crown of beauty for ashes.

- He gives us the oil of gladness for mourning.

- He gives us a garment of praise for despair.

JOURNAL PAGE

Yielding

Teach me, Jesus, how to pray
more like you, have your way.
Create the words within my heart,
so from my lips they do impart.
Teach me in the silent hour,
to wait upon your strength and power.
Mold my life like yielding clay
in your footsteps, every day.
Jesus Christ, ever so sweet,
with nail scarred hands and feet,
I bury old self with you this day
and resurrect in power, *your way.*

—*Yvonne Martinez*

JOURNAL PAGE

Chapter 6

DANCE OF FORGIVENESS

"Give, and it will be given to you. A good measure,
pressed down, shaken together and running over,
will be poured into your lap. For with the measure you
use, it will be measured to you."
—Luke 6:38

The Dance of Surrender and The Dance of Forgiveness are necessary for authentic intimacy with Him. They reveal dependency, love and trust, keeping our hearts pure. A life of surrender and forgiveness can follow the lead of the King. These two dances are the antidote for anger, rebellion, offence, and bitterness.

JOURNAL PAGE

Forgiveness is a fruit of surrender. Those who surrender their lives to God choose to forgive, not because they should, but because they want to. Forgiveness is the courage to let mercy triumph over judgment (James 2:13).

God provided forgiveness for people who were destined to fail but who chose to return to God. In the Old Testament, sin was forgiven through sacrificial offerings. Then God sent his son, Jesus, who for all time *is* the sacrifice for our sins. It is through Jesus we have forgiveness, and because we have been forgiven we can forgive others.

In forgiving, we release our judgment or desire for revenge. Inpatient hospital programs advertise "Forgiveness Therapy" and an employee from a major corporation recently told me it had scheduled "Personal Enrichment" seminars (which included the topic of forgiveness) to increase self-esteem and productivity of employees. These programs are finding out what God has told us all along—there is a connection between forgiveness and good mental health.

Forgiveness was God's idea so it is no surprise we have many Biblical examples and instructions about God's forgiveness or our forgiving others.

JOURNAL PAGE

In fact, *Strong's Exhaustive Concordance of the Bible (NIV version)* lists 102 verses that use the words *forgive, forgiven,* or *forgiveness! (NIV version)*

In Matthew 18:21-35, Jesus tells us a parable about a master who cancels a great debt owed by his servant. The servant, in turn, refuses to extend mercy to his debtor. When the master learns about this, he becomes angry and turns the servant over to be tortured until he pays back all he owed. Then Jesus says, *"This is how my heavenly Father will treat each of you unless you forgive your brother from your heart."*

We have been released from a great eternal judgment for our sins, given a new birth, the Kingdom and eternal life. God wants us to forgive because He has forgiven us. He wants us to show mercy because He has shown us mercy. Extending mercy is no longer desiring that others will get what they deserve.

Giving forgiveness to those who hurt us

When we experience the grace of God's forgiveness we forgive others more freely. We choose to release from our judgment those who have hurt us, and we choose to show mercy toward them. Releasing others from our prideful judgment releases us from the pain

JOURNAL PAGE

and emotional torture unforgiveness produces. When we forgive, God releases us and we release ourselves.

Think of a fish caught on a hook. As the fish struggles and struggles, the hook penetrates deeper into the fish. As long as the fish focuses on the fisherman and the struggle, the hook twists and turns in its flesh. The struggle causes more pain for the fish than for the fisherman. When the fish forgives, it cuts the line and stops the struggle with the fisherman. Forgiveness sets the fish free. Afterward, the fish can get the hook out allowing the wound to heal.

Giving forgiveness to those who are not sorry

Often we want to set up conditions or see remorse on someone's part before we will forgive them. Sometimes we want them to "suffer the consequences" of their behavior so we withhold forgiveness. This really means our forgiveness is conditioned upon the guilty party's repentance. We say, *"If you're sorry, I'll forgive you."* Jesus says, *"I forgive you,"* which causes us to feel sorry. Jesus' forgiveness and mercy invites our repentance. When we forgive, we let go of our connection to their behavior. This actually allows the other person freedom to wrestle with their heart issues.

JOURNAL PAGE

Giving forgiveness when you don't feel like it

When hurt hasn't been addressed, forgiveness will seem detached from feelings.

It is like looking into a closet that has been cluttered for a long time. Every time you open the closet door you see the mess and feel bad. You will never enjoy the good feelings that come from having a clean closet while you are still looking at the mess. Just as soon as you begin working on the mess and the closet is finally clean, the good feelings of relief and release come naturally.

When you obey God and clean out the clutter of unforgiveness, you are drawn closer into the next dance —the Dance of the Overcomer.

Giving forgiveness to those who persist in abusing you

Whoever hurts you or abuses you, a Christian, is guilty of sin against God's temple (1Cor. 3:16; 6:19). Allowing them to continue hurting you is not good for them and, of course, not good for you. In every case that Jesus endured or submitted to persecution, it was to bring glory to his Father. Likewise, our submission

JOURNAL PAGE

should bring glory to God or cause others to be drawn to Christ.

When David (1 Samuel) was persecuted and pursued by Saul, he removed himself from the violence. On two occasions, David spared Saul's life when he could have killed him in defense. If David had retaliated, he would have been no better than Saul. David was able to leave Saul in God's hands, and God honored David.

Relationships that continue to damage you emotionally or physically need to be handled with the same maturity. You can remove yourself from the abuse and the abuser. Forgiveness doesn't mean you can or should continue in relationship with people who aren't safe or who aren't trustworthy.

Giving forgiveness when you are angry

Being angry is not a sin, but extended hostility, insult, or injury is. Anger has active expressions like yelling, throwing things or hitting people. It also has passive expressions like forget-fullness, procrastination, or apathy. You know anger is a sin when you see its negative responses and reflection in the faces of others we have hurt.

JOURNAL PAGE

Asking forgiveness for our offenses

When we confess our sins (and unforgiveness is a sin), God will forgive us. This forgiveness is guaranteed through Jesus. When possible, we also need to ask for forgiveness from those we have directly or indirectly hurt.

Asking for forgiveness when someone refuses to forgive

Your asking for forgiveness is an act of obedience and shows responsibility as well as maturity, but you cannot dictate what the response might be. The act of asking for forgiveness releases the one you've wounded. Your asking for forgiveness cuts the line from you, the fisher, to the fish. Your asking for forgiveness gives up your struggle with the fish by you cutting the line and the fish is set free. How they handle their freedom is not your responsibility.

Receiving forgiveness for our offenses

If we don't forgive ourselves, we haven't truly believed God has forgiven us and we continue to punish ourselves for the things Christ died for. This action tells

JOURNAL PAGE

God that Jesus sacrifice is insufficient payment for our mistakes or sins.

We may have failed but we are not a failure. We cannot do anything to remedy our shame and guilt. Jesus alone can remove them through His atonement. There is a cleansing (1 John 1:9) and healing (Ps. 103:3 and Ps. 147:3) element associated with God's forgiveness. The purity of Jesus' shed Blood washes us, not just covering over, but removing any stain or odor, any residue or evidence. Receiving forgiveness is partnering with God's love.

Unforgiveness

Unforgiveness keeps the door open to the pain of trauma. It also leaves the door open to anger, hatred, bitterness, rebellion, and murder. Unforgiveness is holding an ungodly power against or over someone.

The premise is if resolution or a reduction in intensity of the memory was to take place, then emotional connection would diminish and stop the ability to have control or cease the ability to seek revenge against those who hurt them.

I visited a Christian woman while hospitalized for a nervous breakdown. Five years earlier she had been

JOURNAL PAGE

raped by a man she knew and trusted. When I asked her about forgiveness, she said she would *never* forgive him for what he did. Unforgiveness held open the door to the trauma so she could revisit anytime and find ways for revenge. The open door also allowed him to mentally rape her over and over.

This conversation came to my mind one evening when I was making dinner. Opening a can of tomatoes and pouring them into a pan, I could smell the tomatoes had a bad odor. Looking into the empty container I saw corrosion on the inside of the can. I checked the outside of the can and found it had been dented. I realized the dent caused the contents to spoil.

The Lord showed me that this is how unforgiveness is in our hearts. Our unforgiveness is like acid in a fragile cup. A blow to the outside damages the delicate contents and corrodes the inside of the container.

The forgiver pays a great price and the guilty goes free. This is the example that Christ gave us. He forgave and we go free. There is no other payment for our guilt.

Unforgiveness will never remedy a wrong or fix the problem. Wrong doing, even when forgiven, may

JOURNAL PAGE

have perpetuated consequences that we no longer have the power to control or change. In most cases the emotional or physical damage is either irreparable or irreplaceable. Likewise, we forgive because repayment is impossible and unforgiveness is a death-grip on pain.

What Forgiveness Isn't

Forgiveness is essential to healing, releasing us from the pain of torment. But forgiveness isn't denying the pain, excusing the crime or guaranteeing reconciliation.

Forgiveness isn't denying the pain

Sally was taken into the woods and tortured by a boyfriend. He cut off her arms and wrapped her with duct tape. Sally managed to get to the road and was rescued by a driver. Forgiveness doesn't erase Sally's need for medical attention. Although this is a profound example, it makes the point. The brutal physical wounds from Sally's attack aren't healed when she forgives her attacker. There remains the process of learning how to live her life in the aftermath of this tragedy. Forgiveness is essential, but we may be faced

JOURNAL PAGE

with physical and emotional pain that needs further healing to put lives back on track.

In the fishing scenario, after the line was cut, the hook in the fish still needed to be removed so the wound could heal.

Forgiveness isn't excusing the crime

Jesus acknowledged the repentant thief hanging on the cross next to Him. In Jesus' compassion toward the thief, Jesus told the thief he would be in paradise that day with Jesus (Luke 42:43). However, the thief still died for his crime.

My husband, Tony, led a prison ministry. Every service he ministered to men who were forgiven by Christ, yet who were still serving their sentences. Forgiveness rectifies the spiritual judgment, but it doesn't necessarily absolve from the restitution required according to our moral, judicial or governmental laws.

Forgiveness isn't reconciliation

Forgiving doesn't mean you will, or can, have relationship with the ones you forgive.

JOURNAL PAGE

My father died before I became a Christian. For-giveness couldn't reconcile our relationship, but I have the peace of knowing I let go of my hurt and an-ger. Through Christ, I was able to forgive him for his rejection and abandonment.

In the example of David and Saul, it wasn't safe for David to remain close to Saul (1 Sam. 19:1). David was willing, but Saul's attitude and actions stood in the way of their relationship. If Saul had been willing to change, the story would have had a much different ending.

Forgiveness isn't reconciliation, but it's a beginning

Today's language would describe David as detach-ing himself from Saul and establishing healthy boun-daries. For David, relationship with Saul was never re-established. David remained pure in heart and in 2 Samuel, Chapter 1, David was sincerely grieved at Saul's death and honored Saul for the greatness of Saul's life.

The goal for David, and for us, is to back up, catch our breath, redesign our plan, and merge back into our lives as ambassadors of Christ Jesus.

JOURNAL PAGE

Returning to the fishing metaphor, we need to cut the line, remove the hook, and doctor our wounds. During this process we learn valuable lessons about where the fisher fishes and what bait he uses. Learning healthy boundaries helps to ensure we activate the tools needed for building safe relationships.

Reconciliation with the fisherman may not be possible or safe but we will swim along happier because forgiveness *will* guarantee reconciliation with God.

Anger

Anger, like unforgiveness keeps open connection to the trauma, allowing entry back into the event, reinforcing the bonding. Anger is a futile attempt to control a situation that has been out of control.

Rachel emptied the trash after a party and forgot to lock the back door. Later the evening a man entered the house, sexually assaulted and attempted to rape her.

I first met with Rachel about three months after the attack. Rachel finished the story. During the sexual assault Rachel began to tell the man he didn't have to hurt her because Jesus loved him. The man stopped and ran from the house. With Rachel's help,

JOURNAL PAGE

her identification and willingness to come forward in trial, the assailant was caught and convicted. Rachel felt peace with the way she handled the situation.

Rachel's problem was with her fiancé. He repeatedly questioned Rachel about why she didn't lock the door and continually wanted her to restate exactly what the attacker did to her sexually. He was unable to resolve anger over his fiancé having been sexually violated. Injustice attracts anger, but anger isn't a remedy for injustice.

We also need to resolve the question of anger towards God. It's often easier to forgive a person than to forgive God. After all, God is well aware of the events that happened in our life, and yet, circumstances didn't change. If we become embittered with God we will build a shell of resistance that will insulate us from His presence.

Often I receive calls from someone wrestling with the questions: *"Where was God when this happened and why didn't he stop it?"* I had to personally settle these same questions for myself and so will you.

God is good. God is love. A good, loving God does not order disaster into our life to teach us a lesson. He wasn't out to lunch when bad things happened.

JOURNAL PAGE

God doesn't send us diseases to make us better Christians. The source of affliction is our enemy who uses bad circumstances to build a case of unbelief against God. However, God will use the circumstances to draw us to Him, if we will come.

Jesus suffered and paid the price for our healing and freedom. Jesus was the remedy for God's wrath and the substitute for God's punishment. Jesus took our suffering upon Himself. Jesus died so we could live emotionally, physically, spiritually, and eternally free with full access to the benefits of a good, loving God. If we believe anything less we will create a theology that resists or opposes the truth. Because of Jesus, we are unpunishable.

I couldn't fix myself and neither could any other person. My pain, although not caused by God, created my awareness of need for Him. In retrospect, I can see and experience good that came from the bad. My experiences taught me that I must trust in Him no matter what the circumstances look like.

We live and contend with unanswered mystery. The uncomfortableness of contending with mystery creates doctrines and theologies to soothe our minds.

JOURNAL PAGE

Whatever grace we receive to access doors of revelation is received in relationship with Him. The truth that sets you free will never be found through mental gymnastics or religious principles. So, don't be led through a maze, a journey inward, to find the answers to your problems.

Our minds don't contain the answers, Jesus does. The answer must be found outside of ourselves, in a journey to discover Him.

JOURNAL PAGE

Chapter 7

DANCE OF THE OVERCOMER

The Lord is faithful, and he will strengthen and
protect you from the evil one.
—2 Thessalonians 3:3

We are His chosen, His friend, the object of His affection and attention. The Dance of the Overcomer is taking possession of your position in Him. This is not only freedom from your past but freedom to engage your destiny.

In Song of Songs 2:9,10 the "lover" comes to the "beautiful one" to arouse her from a place of comfort. The lover invites the beautiful one out from behind

Journal Page

her wall to join Him as He, like a gazelle, bounds from mountain top to mountain top, conquering the "high places" signifying His dominion over things that have exalted themselves against the knowledge of God. We join Him as a partner in the Dance of the Overcomer, no longer walking on His feet, but our hand in His hand and close by His side.

For the beloved to accept the invitation to this dance, she must come out from behind her wall.

"But we all, with unveiled face, beholding as in a mirror the glory of the Lord, are being transformed into the same image from glory to glory, just as by the Spirit of the Lord." (2 Cor. 3:19) The veil (any protective covering) needs to be removed so we can go from "glory to glory."

He doesn't break down the wall or rip off the veil. He doesn't kidnap her against her will. Rather, it is a partnership whereby she willingly joins him. Accepting the invitation, He takes her on a journey appearing much like Superman and Jane! He begins to teach her about conquering and overcoming, dominion and authority. These next verses from 2 Corinthians tell me if we are in a war and we have weapons, we must have an enemy!

JOURNAL PAGE

"For though we live in the world, we do not wage war as the world does. The weapons we fight with are not the weapons of the world. On the contrary, they have divine power to demolish strongholds. We demolish arguments and every pretension that sets itself up against the knowledge of God, and we take captive every thought to make it obedient to Christ." (2 Cor. 10:3-5)

The warfare is a spiritual war that began when Satan first rebelled against God and God exiled him from heaven. We are told (John 14:30) that Satan now sits as the prince of this world. An important fact here is that Satan is only a prince and is subject to the King! When Jesus took the keys to hell and death, Satan's reign as prince was trumped by the King's reign!

Jesus destroyed the works of the devil so you would have full access to immunity and authority—life more abundant as described in John 10:10. I love Kris Valloton's statement, *"The purpose of war is victory, the purpose of victory is occupation and the purpose of occupation is inhabitation."* Jesus won the war to give you victory so you could occupy and inhabit the Kingdom *"on earth as it is in heaven"* (Matt. 6:10).

The territory of dominion given to Adam and Eve must have had spiritual boundaries. They were given

JOURNAL PAGE

authority to expand and subdue the earth. This means the land outside the paradise of Eden was not subdued. Adam and Eve were given the authority to overpower, conquer, discipline, tame, and restrain to expand and enlarge the territory of Eden.

Similarly, the promised land of Canaan, the land the Israelites were to inhabit, was left in the hands of giants (Numbers 13:28). The Israelites had to enter and overpower, conquer, discipline, tame and restrain the land before they could occupy, expand, and enjoy its bounty and fruit.

In both these examples, God had given the people the land, commission to move forward, and the authority to occupy. However, in both situations the enemies who previously occupied the land needed to be conquered.

When Jesus resurrected from the grave, He took the keys to hell and death (Rev. 1:18) and gave them to us (Matt. 16:19). The keys were to unlock access to the Kingdom of God so it would be *"on earth as it is in heaven."* In essence, the reinstatement of Jesus' authority to destroy the works of the devil (1John 3:8) has now been passed on to us. We have been given His authority to expand the Kingdom of God on earth

JOURNAL PAGE

and legally take back territory that has been occupied by the enemy.

Land filled with giants or land filled with milk and honey? After exploring Canaan, the men came back with different reports. Caleb was focused on taking possession of the land with confidence saying, "...*for we can do it.*" (Num. 13:30) In contrast, other men shrunk back in fear with a bad report saying the people of the land were of great size and devour those living in it.

Spiritual warfare is taking back the territory and coming into agreement with the good report, *we can do it!* We take back the land given to us—for us *and* our future generations. What feels like an attack is actually enemy resistance because you entered the territory where he has his couch and refrigerator! It is the place he has made his home. We initiate the conflict to assert the dominion and authority of God.

Since it is a spiritual war, natural or "carnal" weapons are ineffective. The shields and swords of the Old Music and Old Dances don't work on a spiritual enemy.

Denying acknowledgment of an enemy is equally unwise as blaming him for everything. However, the

JOURNAL PAGE

warfare is real and persistent. We have a genuine enemy who will push us to fail, shrink back, and fall.

Discipline and self-control aren't enough to change spiritual atmospheres. A good example is the person addicted to alcohol or food. They can stop excess consumption through will power, but the heart will still be hurting and the enemy will still occupy a stronghold. No one can "white knuckle" their way to inner freedom.

Freedom isn't something we *do*; it must be who we *are*. This hits precisely at the core of our enemies attack —the opposition against our identity in Him. It was the source of doubt used against Eve, it was the source of temptation against Jesus in the wilderness, and it was the source of fear that pricked Thomas' orphan heart.

Satan forfeited his relationship with God. He is no longer part of the Kingdom of God. He is no longer in the inner circle of the Angels that surround the Throne. He is no longer in worship and adoration of God. He is separated from God. He wants us to be like him.

Great military strategist plan their offence and defense before firing their weapons. We also learn what fortifies enemy strongholds. In the enemy's game there is no love, no mercy, and no forgiveness. He is a liar and the father of lies (John 8:44).

JOURNAL PAGE

A liar, like a lion, stalks his prey

Satan cannot be everywhere and doesn't know everything. However, he's been around long time and sees us and our world from a different vantage point. He unfairly uses unguarded moments of trauma, fear, hatred, occult or sexual sin. He watches and waits for vulnerability and wounding and the places we have believed lies. He is an opportunist, using the lies against us to strengthen his stronghold.

A liar disguises

He often appears with an approachable demeanor. He came to Eve in the form of a serpent (Gen. 3:1) and as an angel of light (2 Cor. 11:14). When we aren't looking to God to meet our needs, the enemy can become what we think we need.

A liar destroys

He attacks through the circumstances, placing a wedge between Christians and their faith. Satan's goal is to destroy a Christians' relationship with God, their effectiveness and influence.

JOURNAL PAGE

A liar defends

His claim is stacked with doubt, deception, and delusion. His progressive success creates a stronghold, an area of predominance.

A liar plants doubt

Satan's first move against Eve was to plant skepticism or disbelief in her mind about the character of God.

A liar plants deception

Satan uses deliberate concealment or misrepresentation by adding just enough mixture of truth to make it palatable. He told Eve, she would *"be like God, knowing good and evil"* (Gen. 3:4). She *was* already like God in that she was made in His image AND she *would* very quickly know good and evil. These were truths he twisted to manipulate.

A liar plants delusion

Satan wants to deposit his rebellion and self-will. Eve's belief (agreement) she needed what Satan's lie

JOURNAL PAGE

offered rendered her unable to detect falsehood or make sound judgment.

A liar fears truth

His loss comes when his tactics and defense, built on lies, is shattered by the Spirit of Truth. Satan's stronghold is camped in the mind of those who don't know who they are in Christ Jesus. That is why we are to *"be transformed by the renewing of our minds."* (Ro. 12:22)

Underneath the lie is a wound, a hurtful place, and when the demonic has encapsulated both the wound and the lie, it shields the lie from the truth. I know ministries that make the mistake of trying to tackle wounds, lies, and demons with the same approach. Healing of wounds, exposure of lies, and abolishment of demons are different issues and need to be approached from different strategies.

If you make a fist with one hand and then tightly place your other hand over the fist, you have a visual of what I mean. The fist is the wound. The other hand is the enemy encircling the wound. The magnet holding the enemy attached to the wound is the lie. If

JOURNAL PAGE

deliverance methods are used on wounds, more trauma or spiritual abuse is possible. Additionally, it is ineffective to counsel a demon! You don't heal a demon and you don't deliver a wound. Wounds need healing and demons are eliminated through deliverance.

At the core between a wound and the demonic is a lie, like mayonnaise between two slices of bread! In 2 Cor. 10:5 we are told to demolish arguments and every pretension that sets itself up against the knowledge of God and to take captive every thought to make it obedient to Christ. While the demonic is in direct opposition to God, it uses the lie to exalt itself against God. When the lie gets dissolved, the wound can be separated from the demonic and dealt with accordingly. John 8?32 reminds us that when we know the truth, the truth will set us free.

The Dance of the Overcomer is coming out of agreement with the lies and into partnership with Jesus as a "son" and an "heir."

Handling Our Thoughts

Being confronted by our thoughts and feelings isn't necessarily negative. The source can be promptings from the Holy Spirit leading us into truth or our

JOURNAL PAGE

mind rehearsing conversations or events (self-talk), or the enemy's attempt to throw us off course. Thoughts that linger and persist consume our productivity, demanding our attention. They are usually thoughts that strike a vulnerable or unresolved emotional area and become a trigger point.

When the thought is persistent, you don't know the source or can't resolve it, challenge it with the following process.

Is this condemnation or conviction?

Condemnation is from the enemy. It produces false guilt with spiritual death as a goal. It overshadows and points to mistakes or sin. Condemnation's motive is an invitation to resurrect the gravesite of your past, returning to relationship with the Old Music and Old Dances.

Conviction is from the Holy Spirit. It produces true guilt with holiness as a goal. It overshadows and points to mistakes or sin. Conviction's motive invites you to surrender the situation to the gravesite and return your focus on the resurrected Christ in you uniting in relationship with Him.

JOURNAL PAGE

Is this temptation or a test?

Temptation is from the enemy. Its goal is sin and separation from God. The attractive package contains handcuffs. If you indulge, the attraction will turn to distraction and condemnation will scream accusations.

A test is from God. Its goal is Christian character and draws us closer to God. Tests are often lessons in stewardship. They don't always feel good but ultimately work for our good.

Resolution

If the thoughts are from Old Music or Old Dances and have been surrendered, you've asked for forgiveness and you have forgiven others, then stand firm, rejecting the lie.

If you are not sure, pray about it immediately. Resolve the guilt by accepting any of your personal responsibility. Ask and receive God's forgiveness.

If it is something you are not responsible for, then place responsibility where it belongs then surrender and forgive. Resist and stand firm, rejecting the lie.

You can keep a journal with dates as a memorial to your journey in healing.

JOURNAL PAGE

Discerning the voice of the Good Shepherd is important. Jesus tells us that we will know His voice (John 10:14). Discernment protects you from receiving a false comforter or self-protective behavior which is a lie baited with pain, stress or fear, etc.

The voice of the Good Shepherd will always *lead* you. The voice of another will *drive* you. Refuse to follow the voice of "another." Allow the Spirit of Truth, who is in you, to keep your motives pure. Being tempted does not mean you are sinning. Remember, Jesus was tempted and refuted the lies with truth.

Learn your trigger points. What are the circumstances that cause you to lose your peace? If you feel triggered, a key is to ask God to show you what He wants you to know about yourself and that situation. Then surrender, forgive and renounce any lies, receive His truth.

Revelation opens the door to access. I love the promise at the close of Matthew 14:35-36, *"And when the men of that place recognized Jesus, they sent word to all the surrounding country. People brought all their sick to him and begged him to let the sick just touch the edge of his cloak, and all who touched him were healed."* When we recognize Jesus, we touch him, and we are healed.

JOURNAL PAGE

Chapter 8

DANCE OF THE KINGDOM

"Now unto him who is able to do immeasurably more than all we ask or imagine…"
— Ephesians. 3:20

Imagine you are driving a car and spending all your time looking into the rear view mirrors, focusing on where you have been rather than looking ahead through the windshield to where you are going. It is safer and more productive to know where we are going. The past is a road mark which you have already passed by. It is a good reference point but a bad place to park the car!

JOURNAL PAGE

God partnered with us in our past so we could partner with Him in our future. When you partner with God in the Dance of the Kingdom, you are fulfilling Paul's exhortation to leave our past behind and press on toward the higher calling in Jesus (Phil. 4:13,14). Partnering with God *is* taking our seat in Heavenly places with Christ Jesus (Eph. 2:6) with full access to our identity and inheritance in Jesus. When you move forward, the Holy Spirit clears the windshield so you can freely pay attention to your future and fulfill your destiny.

The surrendered, forgiven, overcoming heart following His lead can hear the things of God and realize He is releasing them into the realm of the impossible. In practical terms this means God didn't save, heal, and deliver you so you could just go to Heaven. He gave you a assignment—to demonstrate the will of God, here and now, through His radical power and presence.

The Divine purpose of dancing in the Kingdom is to demonstrate His Presence by answering people's hearts and prophesying their destiny.

God has not kept His mysteries a secret. He has not hid them from us but rather He has hid them *for* us (Prov. 25:2). Jesus' ministry was a model, a

JOURNAL PAGE

live demonstration. Jesus showed us how the Dance of the Kingdom works with His Papa as a partner. He did it through performing miracles, healing the sick, raising the dead, casting out demons, and cleansing the leper. Then Jesus made a profound statement that commissioned us to do the same (Matt: 10: 7,8). He told us we would do even do greater things. *"I tell you the truth, anyone who has faith in me will do what I have been doing. He will do even greater things than these, because I am going to the Father"* (John 14:12).

Have you prayed for someone who is sick and seen them healed? Have you prayed for someone who is tormented and seen them delivered? I have and there is nothing more gratifying than knowing we are plugged into the true source of love and power.

In a recent meeting I had a Word of Knowledge about scoliosis. Two ladies came forward for prayer. One had been in a severe auto accident many years earlier (trauma) and when we prayed her arm lengthened, the pain vanished and her spine straightened! The other lady had pain in her back and one leg was almost 1½ inches shorter than

JOURNAL PAGE

the other. We prayed and her leg lengthened and the back pain was gone!

When you begin this amazing Dance of the Kingdom it will awaken a desire for more and simultaneously require full dependency on God. Even Jesus said *"the Son can do nothing of Himself"* (John 5:19). So when God commissions us to do what Jesus did, we follow suit in knowing that we are incapable without the Father's help.

God is actually interested in your desires and dreams. Paul called it "co-laboring" with Christ (2Cor. 6:1), partnering in the work of Heaven. God's will co-laboring with man's will is seen in Genesis 2:19. God created the animals and then God gave Adam responsibility for naming them.

God didn't hang out and micro-manage Adam, give him hints or try to influence his decisions. God had full confidence in Adam's ability. Naming the animals was more significant than coming up with a word used to identify them. Naming the animals was assigning their character and nature. God created then Adam created. Together they displayed the model of co-laboring. Co-laboring with God means, with joined creativity, you can influence a fallen world.

JOURNAL PAGE

God is creative. He creates. It is who He is and what He does! He created man in His image and inherent in that image is the desire to create. When we create we are most like our Father. He created the original and we become imitators, illustrators of His nature, drawing attention to the true original.

All my life I was creative but creativity had been silenced and stolen by Old Music and Old Dances. The death of creativity is part of the enemies plan to destroy the desire to live and breathe outside the box of religion. I saw this first hand in the country of Russia. The people had lived so long under the strict Communist reign that when they were finally able to build free enterprise they didn't know how. They were bound and afraid and I heard many of them petition for the return of Communism that originally provided work and places to live. They wanted freedom but weren't willing to pay the price to keep it. Freedom will cost you something to embrace it, activate it, and then to give it away. It will require moving forward.

Desire, according to Proverbs 13:12, is a *"tree of life."* The revelation of co-laboring with God

JOURNAL PAGE

and discovering our ideas, talents, gifts and dreams are an expression of Him generates a desire and a passion for life. The element of co-laboring in creativity has become one of my passionate subjects!

In discussing creativity with a worship leader, he asked me to help one of the congregants. Apparently during worship the person would draw cartoons and the worship leader found this to be somewhat disrespectful and distracting. I watched to see what was happening. As if on cue, when worship began the cartoonist began drawing. The man's face and pencil moved with expression and flow. There was definitely something more going on. Later I explained that worship is a creative expression and the person was naturally expressing creativity, which is a form of worship. It was the person co-laboring in expressive adoration of our creator.

Wisdom is a creative craftsman, a co-laboring, Spirit of God according to these excerpts from Proverbs:

"The Lord brought me forth as the first of his works, before his deeds of old; I was appointed from eternity, from the beginning, before the world began…. Then I was the

JOURNAL PAGE

craftsman at his side. I was filled with delight day after day, rejoicing always in his presence...For whoever finds me finds life and receives favor from the Lord." (Prov. 8: 22-35)

I think it is pretty wild that Wisdom is the Creative Spirit of God. It opens the door to realize that co-laboring in creativity is more than artistic expression. Wisdom creates inventions, technology, governmental institutions, administrations, social systems, engineering, architecture, science, medical breakthroughs, and so on.

We expand the territory of God by releasing what He has given us and demonstrating who we are called to be, His friends. Jesus said, "*I no longer call you servants, because a servant does not know his master's business. Instead, I have called you friends, for everything that I learned from my Father I have made known to you*" (Jn. 15:15). We are God's friend. Friends talk, share, commune, laugh and cry together. They share dreams, ideas, and plan to spend time together. Friendship is greater than servanthood but it doesn't replace it. Friends are the greatest servants of all because they serve out of love not out of duty.

JOURNAL PAGE

As friends of God, our inheritance of wisdom and creativity is to be released to the world. What would it be like to have ideas that would transform business, governments, or nations? What are your dreams, your desires? The answers to these two questions could beautifully merge to create a world changing influence.

Sometimes when we day dream or our mind wonders it is actually God taking us on a revelatory adventure. The co-laboring adventure may be for you or for someone else. It releases you into the prophetic—hearing from God for the people.

A young couple caught my attention and as I watched them I had thoughts that they were going to travel internationally. I felt as though they would carry a great influence where they went and would impact a people group. When I spoke this to them, they began to cry. They were both in law school studying international law. Their goal was to use international legal systems to rescue children from the slave trade. He used me to tell them He saw their dreams and desires and used revelation to prophesy a confirmation they were on the right track.

JOURNAL PAGE

Receiving Kingdom revelation is not something you can muster up through good works or attending church. This is why surrender and forgiveness are so important. The Holy Spirit descended on the Lamb of God and remained giving Truth, Comfort and Counsel. *"And the Holy Spirit descended in bodily form like a dove upon Him, and a voice came from heaven which said, You are My beloved Son; in You I am well pleased"* (Luke 3:22). Tenderness of heart yielded in "son-ship" unlocks Gods mysteries and revelation is ushered in by the Holy Spirit.

The Dance of the Kingdom requires tuning in to His station. It is watching, listening, and moving with Him to display His power. When we purpose to focus on Him we find out He has great things to say! He is passionate about you and me. He has our picture on His refrigerator!

The road into the Kingdom of God is narrow as explained in Matt. 7:14, *"But small is the gate and narrow the road that leads to life, and only a few find it"*. However, once you are inside it is an adventure in *"righteousness, and peace, and joy in the Holy Ghost"* (Rom. 14:17). Life inside the Kingdom is an extraordinary partnership dance with Him! I really like the "joy" part!

JOURNAL PAGE

Chapter 9

DANCE
FACE TO FACE

*"Come! Whoever is thirsty, let him come; and whoever
wishes, let him take the free gift of the water of life."*
—Revelation 22:17

Spiritual hunger can be satisfied by one thing—
His Presence. The intimacy of God's presence fulfills
all desire. Haggai 2:7 speaks prophetically of the *"desire of all nations will come, and I will fill this house with
glory."*

In the King James translation of Romans 8:19,22
Paul says the *"whole creation groaneth and travaileth in
pain together until now"* Bible commentators Jamison,

JOURNAL PAGE

Fausset and Brown (Blue Letter Bible) add this amplification. *"It was enslaved, and the better self longed to be free; every motion of grace in the multitudinous heart of man was a longing for its Deliverer...every sigh from out of its manifold ills, were notes of the one varied cry, 'Come and help us.' Man's heart, formed in the image of God, could not but ache to be reformed by and for Him..."*

Jesus fulfills the desire of man's longing. It isn't doing something for Him or Him doing something for you. It is *being* with Him without barriers. *"And we, who with unveiled faces all reflect the Lord's glory, are being transformed into his likeness with ever-increasing glory, which comes from the Lord, who is the Spirit."* (2 Cor. 3:18) It is our "unveiled face" that reflects His glory. Intimacy is transparency. One of our pastors at Bethel, Danny Silk, says intimacy can be defined as *"into me you see."*

Everything is to lead us into His embrace—the resting place of His Presence. The dance of a lifetime is the intimate Dance Face to Face. Being present with His Presence is a spiritual encounter with the King of Kings.

Kneeling at the foot of the Cross in prayer I experienced Jesus' Blood washing over me. In my spirit, I continued to look up toward Heaven acknowledging

JOURNAL PAGE

redemption and love. Instantly the Blood turned into streams of glitter, gold dust, jewels, colorful confetti, and flashes of light. I felt the Lord tell me these were gifts through His Blood and they were free. He said I could have as many as I want. Yes, I was greedy and began to reach for as many as I could grab hold of. I was having a great time focusing on all the presents from Him.

In the midst of my reaching I felt a hand touch mine. When I looked again, it was the hand of the Lord, taking hold of my hand. He began to lift me to my feet and bring me higher up, past the Blood, past the Cross, and past the Gifts. He brought me up to His Face and looked into my eyes. It was then I realized that the Blood, the Cross, the Gifts were all for this one moment…that I would see His Face. Nothing else matters. The presents were a means to get me to His presence, an intimate experience with Him.

My spiritual dad, Ernie Rogers, told me a story about news journalist and CBS anchorman, Walter Cronkite, who presented a commentary (1960's) on the Baptism in the Holy Ghost. Mr. Cronkite interviewed those who were filled with the Holy Spirit, manifested His Presence through bodily expression (Holy rollers), spoke in unknown tongues, and prayed

JOURNAL PAGE

with people, performing miracles, and the sick were healed. He confirmed they had a genuine experience. Mr. Cronkite also interviewed those who were against the indwelling of the Holy Spirit and speaking in unknown tongues. They gave their theological contentions, negated the fruit and effectiveness. The journalist confirmed they had a genuine argument.

Walter Cronkite reported both sides of the story. At the close of his presentation he said there were genuine experiences and genuine arguments. Then he said something like, I don't know about you, but I'd rather have an experience than an argument!

My last 4 years at Bethel Church has exposed me to the supernatural work of God. At first I had what I called "spiritual whiplash." I had never seen God move in miraculous power—blind eyes opened, deaf ears opened, broken bones healed, tumors disappeared, pain and infirmity gone, emotional breakthroughs, instant deliverance from depression and oppression.

In Mexico on a Bethel School of Ministry mission trip we encountered an 18 month old baby girl whose legs were twisted and curled. My friend, Kay, prayed for the baby and the baby's legs began to straighten.

JOURNAL PAGE

By the end of the meeting the baby's legs were healed and she was learning to walk for the first time. Bethel Church keeps a testimony archive filled with stories of the miraculous.

Just as significant is the paradigm shift I experienced in God healing emotional distress and wounds. My earlier years of ministry included revelation and the prophetic but those gifts were always combating the popular emotional healing processes, programs, and recovery approaches. I still think maturity is a process but I see God moving more quickly and thoroughly in the arena of emotional breakthrough.

My first dentist appointment as a child was really bad. I had lots of cavities and the dentist had no patience. The dentist yelled at me and forced my hands on the chair arms while he worked on my teeth. I complied but was paralyzed with fear. All these years I have hated going to the dentist. I would spend so much time praying before and during appointments and tried all kinds of mental games to calm myself down. A few visits ago I was sitting in the dreaded chair, tears streaming down my face. Believe me, I have forgiven the dentist, the dental assistant, the dental office receptionist, my mom for taking me there and any one else associated with the dental industry!

JOURNAL PAGE

This time I finally asked the Lord "What is up with this?" This time I waited for an answer! I closed my eyes and felt Him show me a picture of myself as that little girl terrified in the dentist chair. I saw the picture of Jesus sitting in the dentist chair and I was in His lap. His arms were wrapped around me and His hands were over mine on the chair arms. My small head rested back against His broad chest as the dentist worked on my teeth. I heard Him tell me was taking care of me that He gently held my hands down so I would be safe. Right after this experience I felt peace and His Presence. All the nervous shaking left my body and I actually felt calm. My current dentist completed the procedure that day and I felt no anxiety or discomfort. I have had other dentist visits since then and although it still isn't my favorite thing to do, I didn't feel nervous or fearful.

In the Transformation Center at Bethel Church where I am on Pastoral Counseling Staff, we see physical healing accompanying emotional healing. Through Bethel Sozo, and encounters with Him, people are emotionally healed and set free in one step!

Many times our physical body is the scene of the crime committed against us. We can hold in our body

JOURNAL PAGE

the residual effects of trauma. For example it can be common to see women who have been sexually abused continually struggle with bladder infections and painful menstrual cycles. When the power and presence of God comes and there is an emotional release we also press in for the physical healing and see mind, emotions and body healed.

Pastor Bill Johnson says any revelation from God's Word that doesn't lead us into an encounter with God only serves to make us more religious. The Church cannot afford 'form without power' for it creates Christians without purpose.

It is the Holy Spirit that brokers Heaven's encounters. He is available to those who follow in faith. Experiencing profound encounters with God should be part of the normal Christian life.

Knowing truth sets you free, but truth should lead us into revelation; the Kingdom realized. *"The kingdom of God is not in word but in power."* (1 Cor 4:14-20)

Kingdom power is inside of you in the form of the Holy Spirit as Jesus told us in Luke 17:21 *"For behold, the kingdom of God is within you."* Also, *"he will be with you forever"* (John 14:16). Then, in John 14:17, Jesus

JOURNAL PAGE

said the world cannot see or know Him, but we know Him *"for he lives with you and will be in you."*

Jesus, in John 14:17, used two examples of the Holy Spirit's presence—*with* us and *in* us. The Holy Spirit is both around us and in us signifying His presence both external and internal.

In my third year of Bethel School of Supernatural Ministry I interned with Bonnie Johnson. Accessing His Presence through the internal Kingdom of God is a passion of hers and she helped me to understand it better.

The external Kingdom is experienced when we enter into an atmosphere of worship or sit under the anointing of a leader and we are affected by the Presence of God around us. "Soaking" was the term used to describe lying down quietly and allowing the external atmospheric Presence of God to penetrate into our spirit. Think of grandma's pickling methods! The vegetables took on the taste and smell of the solution it soaked in.

When we learn to experience the internal Kingdom we access the "living water" Jesus gives so we will never be thirsty again (John 7:38). *"Whoever believes in me, as the Scripture has said, streams of living water will*

JOURNAL PAGE

flow from within him." Jesus told the Samaritan woman (John 4:10), *"If you knew the gift of God and who it is that asks you for a drink, you would have asked him and he would have given you living water."* Then Jesus tells her (vs. 38) for those who believe in Him, the same streams of living water would *"flow from within him."* The unending source of the Kingdom inside us goes with us wherever we go. It is accessible and available to be poured out to others.

He is both approachable and able to be captured. It is possible to position ourselves for an encounter with God. We do this by recognizing the signs of His presence. When He lifts the curtain of our senses to perceive Him, we have entered the Dance Face to Face.

Number 6:26-26 says, *"the Lord make His face shine upon you and be gracious to you."* In conjunction we are told in Matt: 5:16 *"In the same way, let your light shine before men, that they may see your good deeds and praise your Father in heaven."* When God's face shines on our face, we become reflectors of His Glory to others. We have an encounter so we can be an encounter to others. It is the giving away of who we *are*.

"Then Mary took about a pint of pure nard, an expensive perfume; she poured it on Jesus' feet and wiped his feet

JOURNAL PAGE

with her hair. And the house was filled with the fragrance of the perfume." (John 12:3) It is most likely as Mary poured out the perfume it dripped or splashed on her hands, arms and clothing which probably offended the crowd even more! She didn't let the taunts and criticism stop her from pouring and smearing the perfume on Jesus allowing whatever overflow to inadvertently drip onto her. Interestingly, the word "Christ" means *anointed one* and is actually translated "to smear." When we press into Him and step past the religious spirit, we, too will be smeared with the anointing of the Holy Spirit. And the fragrant scent of His Presence will be a sign we have been with Him.

So, my friend, it's time to let go and forgive and move forward. The stage is set. Let the curtain of Heaven open. Put flowers on the graves and say "*goodbye.*" He has arrived. Dance with Him. Dance on the graves of your past. Dance in His Kingdom, dance in His arms, dance while gazing into His face. Dance tenderly, dance in joy, dance wildly, dance with happy feet. Dance like no one is looking then dance for the world to see.

He is here... "*May I have this dance?*"

JOURNAL PAGE

"*...as the movement grew yet swifter, the interweaving yet more ecstatic, the relevance of all to all yet more intense, as dimension was added to dimension and that part of him which could reason and remember was dropped farther and farther behind that part of him which saw, even then, at the very zenith of complexity, complexity was eaten up and faded, as a thin white cloud fades into the hard blue burning of the sky, and a simplicity beyond all comprehension, ancient and young as spring, illimitable, pellucid, drew him with cords of infinite desire into its own stillness. He went up into such a quietness, a privacy, and a freshness that at the very moment when he stood farthest from our ordinary mode of being he had the sense of stripping off encumbrances and awaking from trance, and coming to himself.*"

C.S. Lewis, Perelandra, excerpt from pp. 218-219

For more personal help you can experience the healing journey with Yvonne's Dancing on the Grave of Your Past companion workbook.

Additional Ministry

Dancing on the Grave of Your Past
Experience the healing journey companion workbook

Support Group Facilitator's Guide

More information at
www.StillwaterLavender.com

Bethel Church information www.ibethel.org
Bethel Sozo information www.bethelsozo.com

ABOUT THE AUTHOR

Yvonne is an author, conference speaker, third-year Bethel School of Supernatural Ministry graduate, and hosts articles and Q/A column for the Christian Quarterly entitled *Talk With Yvonne.*

With 25 years experience in prophetic counseling and pastoring, emotional healing and trauma resolution, Yvonne serves on Pastoral Counseling staff in the Transformation Center at Bethel Church in Redding, CA. She also ministers with the Bethel Sozo team and is part of their mentoring program.

As an ordained minister, Yvonne's passion is to see people acquire their Kingdom identity, inheritance, intimacy and authority. She is available for speaking or personal ministry.

Yvonne is the author of:

Dancing on the Graves of Your Past Workbook

Prophetic Gates

Prayers of Prophetic Declaration

Angel Feathers – Chronicle Heavenly Adventures

CONTACT

Yvonne Martinez

Transformation Center

Bethel Church

933 College View

Redding, CA 96003

(530) 255-2099 x 1921

yvonnem@ibethel.org

or

talkwithyvonne@hotmail.com

Books available at

www.StillwaterLavender.com

If you have a testimony you would like to
share as a result of reading this book,
Yvonne would love to hear from you.

20566759R00137

Made in the USA
San Bernardino, CA
15 April 2015